THE**NEXT**HOUSE

THENEXTHOUSE

publisher

Paco Asensio

Text

Lola Gómez
Cristina Montes (p. 14, p. 70, p. 42, p. 110, p. 166)

Art director

Mireia Casanovas Soley

Graphic design and Layout

Emma Termes Parera, Soti Mas-Bagá

Translation

Bill Bain

2002 © Loft Publications S.L. and HBI,
an imprint of HarperCollins International

First published in 2002 by LOFT and HBI,
an imprint of HarperCollins International
10 East 53rd St. New York, NY 10022-5299

Distributed in the U.S. and Canada
by Watson-Guptill Publications
770 Broadway New York, NY 10003-9595
Telephone: (800) 451-1741 or (732) 363-4511 in NJ, AK, HI
Fax: (732) 363-0338

Distributed throughout the rest of the world by
HarperCollins International
10 East 53rd St. New York, NY 10022-5299
Fax: (212) 207-7654

Softcover ISBN: 0-8230-3203-5
Hardcover ISBN: 0-06-008757-9
D.L.: 19414.02

editorial project

© **LOFT** Publications
Domènech, 7-9 2º 2ª
08012 Barcelona. España
Tel: +34 93 218 30 99
Fax: +34 93 237 00 60

loft@loftpublications.com
www.loftpublications.com

If you would like to suggest projects for inclusion in our next volumes,
please e-mail details to us at: loft@loftpublications.com

We have tried our best to contact all copyright holders. In individual
cases where this has not been possible, we request copyright holders to get in touch with the publishing house.

introduction:

The need to
attribute names
to things is fun-
damental in
order to remem-
ber them, to
identify them
and, definitively,
to be able to
mention them.

The need to attribute names
to things is fundamental in
order to remember them, to
identify them and, definitively, to be able to mention
them. In Macondo, the imag-
inary region Gabriel García
Márquez creates in the novel
*One Hundred Years of Soli-
tude (1967)*, he relates how
everything there was of such
recent creation that most
things were still nameless
and people had to point to
them to talk about them.

The custom of attributing
proper names to houses
originated in the Middle
Ages, an era that personal-
ized houses, just as it per-
sonalized the bell towers of
churches, swords, or can-
nons. In that day, names

had meanings, nothing was
accidental.

The selection of single-family houses presented in this
book is an approximation of
a journey through the many
different proposals that
exemplify and explain the
plurality that the concept has
undergone, the evolution of
domestic space.

Returning to the names of
houses being referred to,
our wish here is to recall
to the mind of the reader
A Room of One's Own,
Virginia Woolf's 1929 essay.
In it, the author proposes,
among other things, a lucid
and enjoyable reflection on
women's intellectual capaci-
ty in relation to that of men.
The reflection leads to a

fateful revelation: that the anonymity of the genius and the creative intelligence of woman throughout history was due to her never having had a room that she could lock or an income of 500 pounds a year in the currency of 1929 Britain.

We should pay attention to the detail that the room in the house of Virginia Woolf's protagonist at least was "in" the house. But in the sixteenth century such a room would have been a rarity for anyone, woman or man. A century would pass before anyone would conceive rooms to which we could go to escape the public eye. It is worth reflecting that houses were always full of people, much more than in our own day, and that an awareness of privacy was unknown. These new domestic spaces came to be called private rooms.

A citation from another book by the same author might be considered here:

Orlando now began a series of very splendid entertainments to the nobility and gentry of the neighborhood. The three hundred and sixty-five bedrooms were full for a month at a time. Guests jostled each other on the fifty-two staircases. Three hundred servants bustled about the pantries. Banquets took place almost nightly. Thus, in a very few years, Orlando had worn the nap off his velvet, and spent the half of his fortune...

But when the feasting was at its height and his guests were at their revels, he was apt to take himself off to his private room alone. There when the door was shut, and he was certain of privacy, he would have out an old writing book, stitched together with silk stolen from his mother's workbox, and labeled in a round schoolboy hand, "The Oak Tree, A Poem". In this he would write till midnight chimed and long after....

Orlando (1929)
Virginia Woolf
*Edition from 1974 by
Penguin Books*

The names of houses that appear here, in our book, have nothing in common that would relate or connect them

THE NEXT HOUSE

with each other. But we may say that in all of them is to be found an importance in solving, from many peculiar points of view, an array of domestic needs imposed by the client's wishes.

Hence, we have considered it proper to include in the book some proposals for houses that have not yet been built and probably never will be. The fact remains that both in the standing house with a name of its own and in the house still in blueprint we find expounded and developed that which is fundamental: the idea of the house.

For centuries, the history of architecture has produced an important legacy of names of houses that are significant in determining the conception

and the evolution of what was held to be domestic.

This book does not aim to revise these valuable works of architecture. Simply, we wish to explain and portray examples of recently constructed or imagined houses that re-explain to us –precisely in this moment of our history– one of the most important themes of living projects: different ways of using the house.

We would go so far as to entertain the notion that, once the application of all the possible techniques and instruments of construction today has been surpassed, what distinguishes some building projects from others is not the designs, in large part the same, for all

that, but the immense variety of ways in which people use their houses.

At times, professors of architecture encourage their students to create a story to explain their projects so as to be able to tell others about them in a simple and entertaining way.

In the pages that follow, too, we may encounter not only names of houses but, probably, a discussion of new and recent stories about houses.

House architecture

GLASS HOUSE Almelo

Architect: Dirk Jan Postel   **Location:** Almelo. Netherlands   **Construction Date:** 1997   **Photographs:** Jordi Miralles

The repetition of a geometric module the size of a single bedroom defines this project.

From the outside, the forms of this single-family house in Almelo, Netherlands, are those of a rather plain container. The repetition of a geometric module the size of a single bedroom defines this project.

This rectilinear mass is of the purest lines and contents. On a rectangular plan, it determines the whole of the architectural framework as well as the distribution of the different interior spaces.

The main street front as well as the sides are wholly faced in etched glass panels like ventilated exterior leaves. This feature conceals the size and position of the different apertures, which remain almost unnoticeable but can be clearly distinguished at night. Only the access porch and the garage door break up the continuity of these walls. By day, the flat glass allows the landscape in which the house is set to cast mirror-like reflections, achieving a full integration with the environment. At night, however, the artificial interior lighting reveals what is happening inside the house.

Although this essential box-like structure is presented as a cold, flat body, it simultaneously opens onto the back garden. On this side, large windows, their dimensions governed by the framing module, comprise the form of communication between interior and exterior. This fluidity is not only visual, it is also physical. The oversize openings act as covered terraces in the winter, left free of curtains, and this often provokes for those inside the sense of being in a kind of gigantic glass case with misty spatial boundaries. The remainder of the façade employs a wood siding that humanizes the coldness of the rationalist forms and offers greater warmth than the street front.

In the interior of the house, a simple svelte stair, visible from the street becomes the key juncture. The downstairs area is used for daytime activities, and includes a garage; the upper story distributes its space among different rooms.

In contrast with the glass that comprises most of the cladding, birch wood has been used as a finishing for the different interior spaces. Translucent glass, however, has been used in the interior doors and is practically the only other material. The textural contrast achieves a kind of balance and well defines the private spaces. It offers a warm comfort that belies the more open, public construction of the colder exteriors.

The cladding on the garden façade is of cedar wood. It is a surface that is highly weather resistant and comes from controlled plantations so that it adapts well to the philosophy of sustainable building.

The terrace and breezeway in the rear open to views of the hills and create a happy, warm setting.

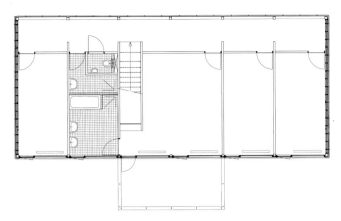

First floor plan

Ground floor plan

The house contains daytime functions on the ground floor and nighttime ones on the upper story. The entrance to the rectangular building marks a main axis between the front and back façades.

The blend of facing materials is intended to enrich the space and integrate it in the surroundings.

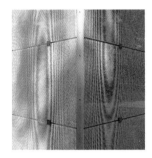

On the garden side, the rear façade provides access to the ground floor of the building, which extends outward in a porch that shades the interior. The first floor is characterized by a "fenêtre en longueur" that includes all the upstairs rooms.

Wood is a major actor in the interior decoration. It warms and welcomes, as witnessed by the birch finishing of the partitions running the length of the space.

The use of birch, a light-toned wood with prominent grain, is not considered uncommon. The tree grows rapidly and is found in abundance in northern and eastern Europe.

The stairway becomes a connector both visually and physically along at least two axes, creating a kind of entrance foyer.

The stairway is intended to be light and transparent, like all of the elements in the house, including doors and windows.

The string of the stairway is a cut of metal which, from above, appears to fold down easily to display the connections.

The interior spaces are bathed in natural light. The glass, wood, and galvanized steel used pay off in quality and comfort.

The finishings inside the house are guided by the general philosophy of design and construction inherent in façades and superstructure. Here, the narrow wall-to-wall mirror and the sliding windows stand out.

BÖHLER-JUTZ HOUSE

architect: Baumschlager & Eberle   **Location**: Dornbirn. Austria   **construction date**: 2000   **photographs**: Eduard Hueber

The formal composition of the building is rather serene and it rests comfortably on its site.

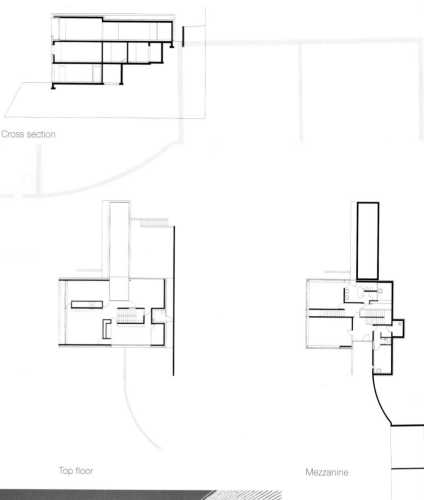

Cross section

Böhler-Jutz House is set on a hill, resting in a landscape, positioned on a sloping site. The history behind the house is not known. It is built on three levels, its rooms distributed according to the degree of privacy desired, and they are accessed separately.

The building is of brick, with windows and doors elegantly framed in metal. Handsomely, the window panes reflect the surrounding environment, even from afar.

On the highest part of the site is a shallow wading pool that marks a boundary with the difference in grade, which drops from one of the long sides of the pool. This same element serves as a lookout point, protected by a glass guardrail that is almost imperceptible.

At the other end of the house, a containing wall on the site curves into a path that leads to the main door of the house. The stepped layout of the house is the natural result of the hillside terracing used as a practical building measure.

The architectural volume is configured like a closed tower of brick of rather compact appearance which, at the same time, is clearly broken by apertures of different but clearly defined dimensions.

The distribution of the rooms has left the more private areas on the ground floor. The higher level includes a landscaped exterior with terrace and pool, and it is also this level that houses the kitchen, dining room, and living room. The bedrooms are on the lower level. Thus, there are two bedrooms on the mezzanine floor, and four more on the ground floor. The ground floor also houses the study spaces or library.

Top floor

Mezzanine

Ground plan

The stepped architecture is the result of the hill slope. The particular hierarchy of the levels establishes common areas at the top of the building and areas dedicated to nighttime activities on the lower floors (including the bedrooms).

A naked HOUSE

architect: Shigeru Ban Architects   **Location:** Kawagoe-shi, Saitama-ken, Japan   **construction date:** November 2000   **photographs:** Hiroyuki Hirai

Some time for meditation is always necessary before
accepting the project for a private residence.

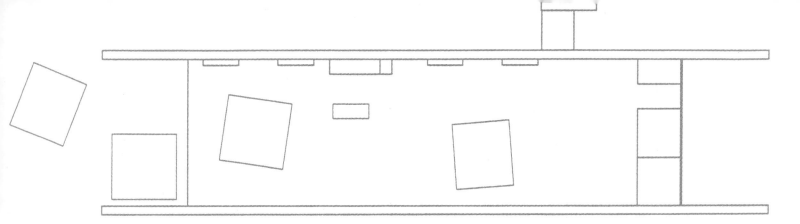

It is always necessary to reflect for a while before accepting the project for a new private residence. Often, without compromising his or her own beliefs, the architect will ask whether what the designer on the project wants is the same as the needs and the desires the clients have for their house.

In the present case, the architect had interviewed the client only once and thus considered clear what the real aims were for the house. The client had stated the precise requisites: a budget of 25,000,000 Yen and the family relationship of those who would live in the building, –the client's mother, himself, his wife, their two kids, and a dog. What he wanted was described as a house providing "enough privacy to be sure the people in the family are not isolated, a house that gives everybody freedom to have individual activities in a shared environment."

The building is close to a river and surrounded by fields with greenhouses. The exterior walls are two panels made of plastic and reinforced fibers, and the nylon fiber inner walls are on a wooden frame. Between both are polyethylene-filled plastic bags that serve as insulation. Through these bags, a pleasant diffuse light penetrates the interior of the house.

The house is a single large space of two stories, with four individual rooms equipped with wheels that can be freely moved. To reduce the weight and optimize mobility, these rooms are small and con–tain a minimum number of objects. They can also be moved according to the needs of their use. They are situated against the walls of the house, in front of the heating and air-conditioning units.

The versatility of these elements makes it possible to place them together and thus create a larger room, eliminating the sliding doors. They can even be taken onto the terrace to take full advantage of the interior space. They can even be used as an additional flooring as a playroom for children. The result is the architect's vision of an agreeable and flexible way of living which evolved out of the client's idea of promoting family life.

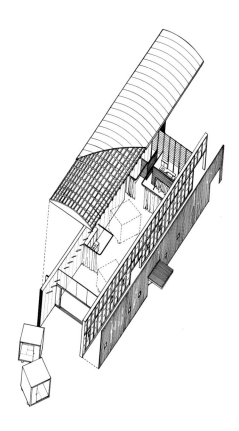

The different containers constitute the desired number of sleeping rooms. The mobility of the pieces allows the dwelling to be used without affecting the "enclosed privacy" of each room.

The house displays a single aspect for different uses and orientations, merely employing the translucent quality of both façades as protection and as a relational element with the exterior.

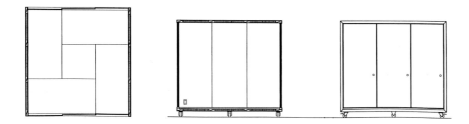

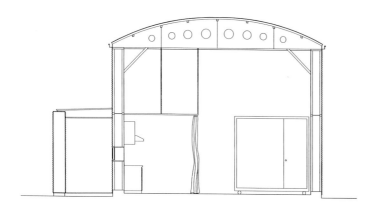

Floor plan distribution of the different stories according to varying decorating proposals for the private-use containers. This mobility can vary at different times of the day, providing the residents with the option of arranging the interior surface area according to the needs of the moment.

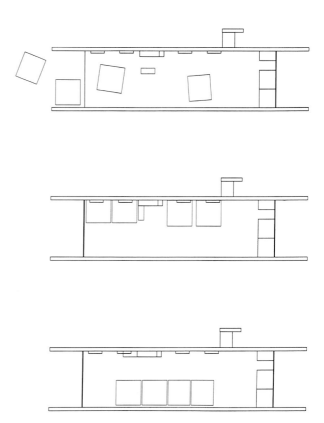

The installations and equipment are concealed in the walls of the house. This basic plan explains the thickness of the two main façades, since the other faces can be considered more like windows that frame the views of the exterior, the only fixed element of this project.

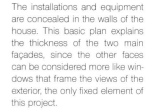

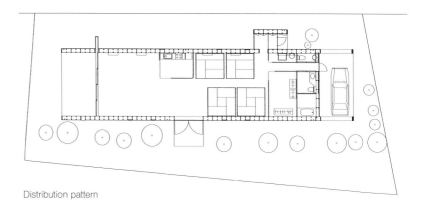

Distribution pattern

the water TOWER

architect: Jo Crepain Architect NV   **Location:** Brasschaat. Belgium   **construction date:** 1997   **photographs:** Sven Everaert

The project consisted of remodeling and shoring up a concrete construction used as a cylindrical water tower.

Based on landscape architect Jan Moereels's commission, the project consisted of remodeling and shoring up a concrete structure used as a cylindrical water tank. The head was supported by four 75-foot columns on a 7,226-square-foot site beside an arroyo at the edge of a wood. These natural geographical features determined the landscape architecture as well as the materials used in the tower. The house in its final version, covered with a native variety of ivy, was to merge with the natural setting.

The 13-foot-high cylinder rests on four columns, which rise 75 feet above the ground. Between the columns, 13-foot-square platforms have been inserted, connected by metal stairs.

Moereels's intention was to offer a new vision of the water tower by making it over into an efficiency apartment, incorporating the inescapable extant platforms. This would be achieved by conserving and emphasizing the structure's original function as an important element in the local environment, using a minimal number of simple building materials.

As to the layout, the house that came out of these ideas required that the sleeping quarters on the ground floor wider than the base of the tower. The columns were completely revealed inside, and the ground floor kitchen and dining room were arranged to open onto the street. The centrally located front door was echoed in back by a terrace over the basement. A double-height ceiling at the back was fitted with an oversize window to take in the magnificent view of the arroyo and the woodland. Over the kitchen, a dressing room also became the TV room; and the master bedroom, on the first platform of the tower, also opens onto a terrace just above the living room. The wall of the bedroom is a galvanized screen that can be moved to allow open-air sleeping. Office space is provided on the second platform; the third contains the guestroom.

The floors inside the house are all of polished cement. The frames of the doors and the windows are matte aluminum. The fourth platform has a small winter garden with local plants such as ivy and honeysuckle. An opening was made in the bottom of the water tank, which is now used for parties and other special occasions.

Different metallic stairways connect the separate levels (8 platforms) with the ground. The three sides of the structure that are visible from the street are covered with Reglit glass. The southern façade uses transparent double-glazed glass. It is also this southern front that enjoys three balconies on different levels, thus offering magnificent views as well as access for window cleaning.

The refurbishing of this structure, and its surprising change in function, make it a textbook example of a "minimal vertical living space."

The austerity of the materials used and the exposed super-structure of the building give an innovative look to the construction's new domestic functions.

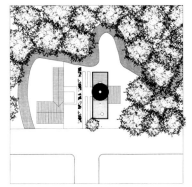

Site plan

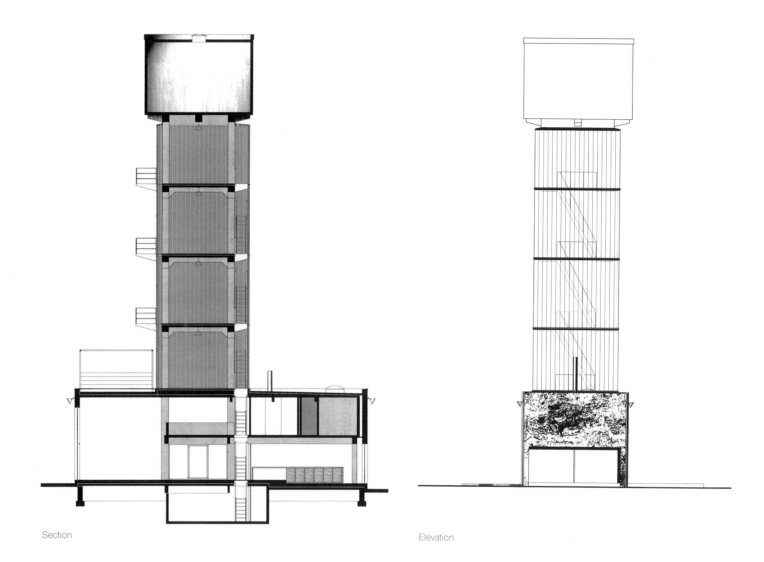

Section

Elevation

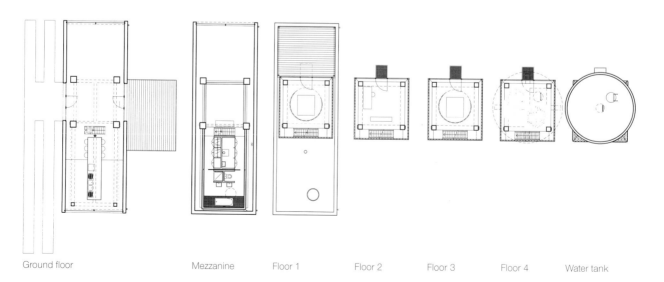

Ground floor   Mezzanine   Floor 1   Floor 2   Floor 3   Floor 4   Water tank

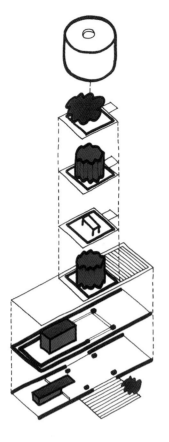

The main room is on the first floor of the cylindrical body, immediately above the living room. This first platform roofs the extension to double-height of the ground floor (where the main and common rooms are kitchen, dining room, living room, guest room).

The rest of the bedrooms are distributed among the other levels. The master bedroom is on the first floor; a second bedroom is on the third floor. Privacy is maintained thanks to sets of circular rails screwed into the ceiling: they serve the curtains circling the bed like old-style canopies.

A view of the inside of the tower with different levels serving different functions.

The sheet-metal stairway between levels is of minimal dimensions and is very light, along the lines of stairs used infrequently or for specific purposes.

red HOUSE

architect: Fulvio Moruzzi **location:** Sitges, Barcelona. Spain **construction date:** 1992 **photographs:** Stella Rotger

Totally integrated into the natural environment of its location, the construction boldly stands between sea and mountain.

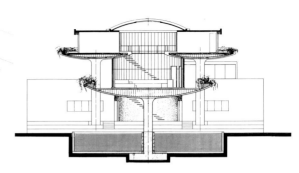

In cross section, the house is defined by its symmetry, which passes un noticed in the finished piece because of the dominant presence of the concrete structure. The cup-shaped capital of the central column serves as protective covering for the pool in the garden.

Ingenious and boastful imagination. That is the best way to define this powerful concrete-and-glass construction by the Swiss architect, Fulvio Moruzzi.

Totally integrated into the natural environment of its location, the construction boldly stands between sea and mountain. The rocky terrain of the Vallpineda Hill in Sitges, Spain, guarantees the dwelling a solid foundation, and the Mediterranean becomes a kind of improvised humble blue carpet at its feet.

The strong visual impact of the building is due to its attractive and unique forms, brought about by the circular elements that contribute to the massive colorist whole. The more than 239 square yards (2,152 square feet) of living space are managed by an aerial platform that uses the terrain to maximum effect. Added to this are three circular structures, each of which is attached at a single point of support. A single central column is topped by a white concrete cup-shaped capital. Of the three, this piece draws the viewer's most immediate attention, overshadowing the matching structures that flank it. Each of these latter two structures has a terrace.

Together, the three structures make up the main frame of the house. The combination of such perfectly fitted geometrical forms creates a spatial tension of great visual strength. The building's verticality is based on a metallic structure of glassed fenestration with the piers painted red (a tone repeated inside). The chimney is painted a gold color and becomes a stabilizing link in the composition. But the three gigantic cups of white are the elements that bring to the mass a subtle horizontality that balances the whole.

On the façade opposite these circular bodies, and on the level of the street, is the main entrance. Beside the front door, still another semicircular element that serves as a canopy juts out from a rounded glass-walled module, like a large mullioned bay window. The back of the site, on the sea side, offsets the main façade by the presence of an imposing pool. Above this is the white concrete cup-capital of the central pillar, reflected, along with other elements, in a shadow play in the water of the pool.

The interiors employ warm colors –red, lime, gold. The contemporary designer fur-

niture maintains the same novel spirit as the exterior, visible from practically every vantage point thanks to the large windows. Thus, along with the spatial communication, there is the added advantage of the natural light flow and the creation of a microclimate inside the house.

The organization of the rooms works on three levels. The lower stories house the common rooms and the upper the private spaces. On the ground floor, taking advantage of the semicircular space formed by the external structure, is a relaxation area like a small amphitheater. The spiral metal staircase originates here, leading to the upper levels and to a walkway that crosses the space to join the rooms on the opposite side.

The organic form of the gigantic concrete columns combines with the glass façades that follow the curvature of the plan. The metallic staircase is extended in a walkway crossing the wide space, the only connection between the two ends of the building.

All the metallic frames are in red, unifying the materials.

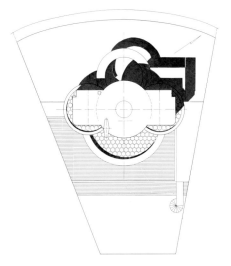

The circular geometry of the plan creates interior spaces that continue up the full height of the building. The top floor is reminiscent of a balcony that opens to the atrium, configured by the spiral staircase.

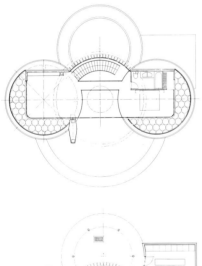

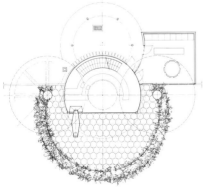

ACHIO HOUSE

Architect: Guillermo Garita, Athanasios Haritos   **Location:** Santa Ana, San José. Costa Rica   **Construction Date:** 1999
Photographs: Oldemar Rivera Quesada, Guillermo Garita (panoramics views), Athanasios Haritos

The building was structured around an interplay between color volumes.

This house, a second residence for a businessman, became a verbal experiment between the architects for the first six months' work, without plans or maquettes. The first models of the project were created precisely as a response to this dialogue. Thus, it took eight months to build the house, after 1,140 hours of supervision.

The project is in Santa Ana, San José, Costa Rica. More concretely, it is in the residential zone of Rio de Oro, an area dotted with small, modest houses. Achio House was a quest for all the previous requisites in the program and for integration into the landscape itself.

A translucent linear barrier defines the garage and protects the southern boundaries. An outer wall protects the site itself and establishes the geometry of a terrain whose northern part situates the house obliquely.

This permits an integration of the dwelling into the environment and relates interior/exterior without compromising the basic premises of protection and privacy. Large mobile panels aid in achieving this aim, and clearly define the entrance zone and dilute the solidity of the plan's distribution.

A skylight filters natural light into the main entrance. The construction is framed on the basis of an interplay of color volumes: red extends the north/south entrance, where the studio is located, and creates privacy without isolation. A walkway connects this mass with the garage.

The house has three gardens: one inside, one outside next to the pool, and what the architects call a "green garden." The roof of the first story is used as a terrace and also serves as spatial referent.

THE NEXT HOUSE

Large mobile panels aid in the exterior/interior integration.

The first six months' work were used to define the functional arrangement of the house. From that point on, the first proposals were started.

First floor plan

Ground plan

Studio floor plan

A walkway connects the structure with the garden and the garage area. A skylight centered on the roof of the ground floor lets natural light into the main entrance.

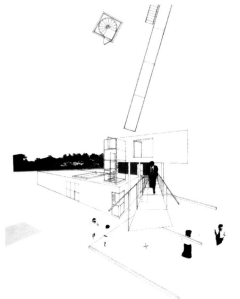

Photographic montage of the last phase of the construction during which the facings of the pool were applied.

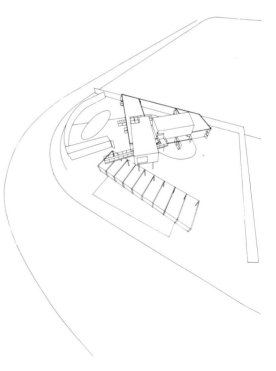

Night view of the house. A peripheral wall protects it and provides privacy.

flatz HOUSE

Architect: Baumschlager & Eberle   **Location:** Schaan. Liechtenstein   **construction date:** 2000   **photographs:** Eduard Hueber

Inside a landscape of houses built in a
traditional rural style, Flatz House rises up uniquely
with a different modern look.

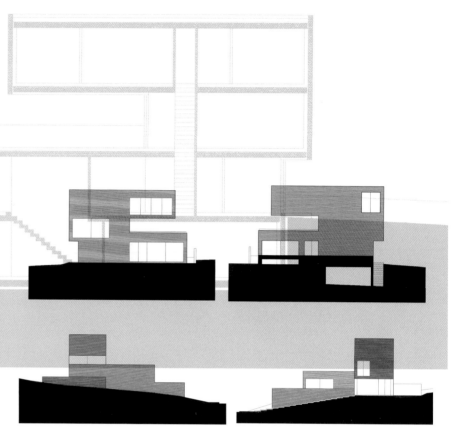

Flatz House is on the gentle west side of one end of the Schaan neighborhood in the Principality of Liechtenstein. It is destined to be the residence of a doctor and his family, made up of seven children.

Immersed in a landscape of houses built in a traditional rural style, Flatz rises up uniquely with a different look. It has the heaviness of piled up building blocks.

The north façade of the house is completely closed, contributing to the compact look of something like a minimalist sculpture. Its hillside siting makes the building unrevealing of what this four-story residence holds. The basement, for example, houses both wine cellar and garage.

The privileged placement of the site was a decisive factor when establishing the criteria of orientating the functional layout of the dwelling. From the highest levels, the eye can look out and see from the Rhine valley to the outline of the Swiss mountains. The living rooms have big windows that set the tone of the paradisal environment. The closure system includes a double glazing that conserves and controls direct sunlight and the possible thermal contrasts that come about in such extreme climates.

The special qualities of the rooms improve with the direct connection with the outdoors. Hence, we see a terrace with a water tank in one corner of the ground floor. On the first floor, the external space is roofed by the façade of the master bedroom. The second floor is designed for use as the children's spaces.

The compact aspect of the house is reproduced in each of the elevations in the drawing.

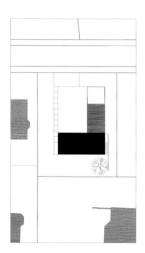

Site plan

The living room opens out to a
gardened terrace that roofs the
lower story.

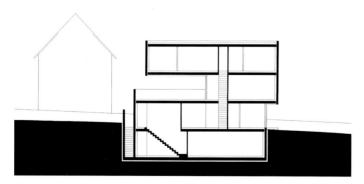

Longitudinal section

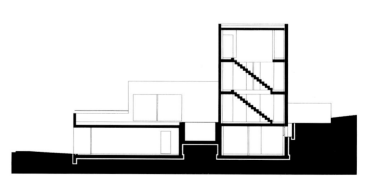

Longitudinal section

Four materials stand out in the construction of the house, elevating the functional features and at the same time the elegance of the architecture. The exterior facings of pigmented cement (corn-colored), the interior finishing (white plastic paint), the plane tree wood features, and the green stone.

shack HOUSE

Architect: Niall McLaughlin Architects   **Location:** Hampshire. UK   **Construction Date:** 1996   **Photographs:** Nick Kane

The history of the place is often the point of departure for architectural discourse. Most projects are born of particular histories.

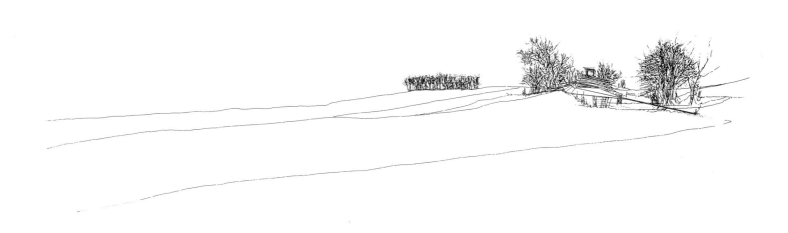

This project is located beside an old lagoon in an agricultural landscape near Kettering. The area was once used as a North American air base during the Second World War. The B-24 bombers would fly over the area on clandestine missions from their place of concealment in the surrounding woodlands in support of the Dutch and French resistance movements. After the war, the site was used as a nuclear missile base until the 1960s. Today, it is sown with the remains of the old war materiel. The history of a place is often the point of departure for architectural discourse. Most projects are born of particular histories.

The owner of Shack House is a photography buff who likes to work against the light. This is the indirect reason why it may be possible to recover the life of the lagoon by oxygenating the water to attract the fauna and the insects that are natural to the bioclimate.

The house is a concrete block with wood and fiber glass pieces that open and extend. Polycarbonate and sheet metal have also been used, reaching out over the water.

Simon Storey was in charge of the construction, and took the job on condition that there would be no cabin design on paper. The work method and the way of con-ceiving it involved myriad maquettes and in situ testing of materials. Storey took charge of the building, started with collages that suggested techniques that could later be used. The whole project design and its construction, in fact, was resolved through maquettes, collages, and photographs as techniques that represented the first "blueprints."

The final form the building acquired is designed to capture and store different types of light.

At the rear of the building, a sloping wall captures light reflected off the lagoon. Superimposed ailerons project changing light plays over the surface.

The roof extends out over the lagoon and the terrain, covered with polycarbonate and perforated sheet metal that evokes a metallic feathering.

Shack House is a refuge for photographer Gina Glover, who specializes in insects. The rest of the family has not been forgotten, however, and her husband has a sauna, and her daughter a recreation room.

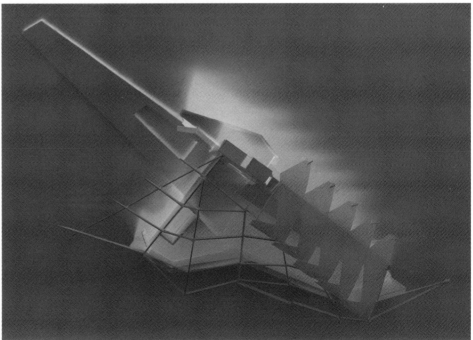

VOS HOUSE

architect: Koen van Velsen   **location**: Amsterdam. Netherlands   **construction date**: 1999   **photographs**: Duccio Malagamba

Trees are one more architectural element with their own space reserved. With this ingenious technique, Van Velsen molds natural light according to his will.

The tree itself is one more architectural element which, like the building's perpendicular lines, breaks up the horizontality of the glass windows.

Beside one of Amsterdam's canals, this Koen van Velsen project is a whole exercise in rationalist mastery and a lesson in neutrality. The building, slotted between two other previously extant buildings, could only move in an upward direction and was thus conceived by the Dutch architect. Van Velsen drew up a totally perpendicular body that plays with large, symmetrical, horizontal apertures, a dynamic with an attractive and provocative visual tension. At its simplest, it is a puzzle.

The brutal inflexibility of the structure's geometries manifests its maximum expression through the materials used: glass and steel. The decision to insert oversize glass apertures, both in the main (street) façade and in the rear (canal) façade, results in the same architectural solution, permitting the creation of totally public interiors. A translucent box which, come nightfall, is transformed by the lighting, lets the curious contemplate the life going on inside the curtainless building.

The continuity of the street façade is interrupted only by the access door to the garage. It is a lifting door, perceived as just another opening when closed, but leading into the parking lot and the vestibule, where a tall tree invades the space from the ground floor to the second story.

The house itself is organized on four levels: basement (with a storeroom, bathroom, studio, and terrace), ground floor (garage access, bedroom, and bathroom), first floor (with a kitchen and dining room), and second floor (living room).

THE NEXT HOUSE

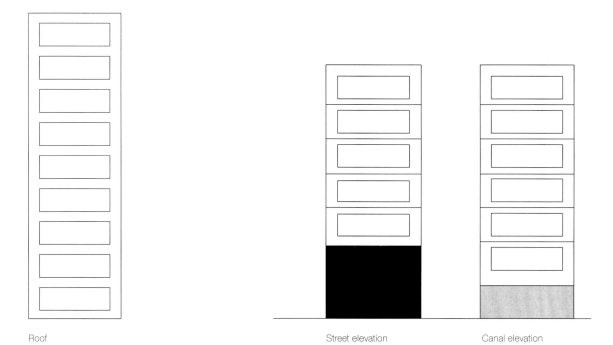

Roof

Street elevation

Canal elevation

The use of different materials in each wall (glass, wood, metal) brings about the articulation of changing spaces.

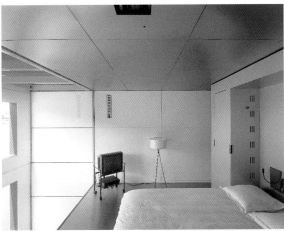

The vertical lines of the stairway respect the transparency maintained transversally throughout the building.

The interior patio becomes the main focus of the house, around which the other rooms develop. But in this case, movement is not horizontal but vertical on all four levels.

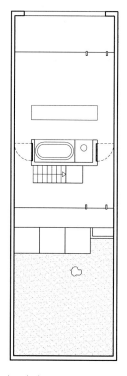

Level -1

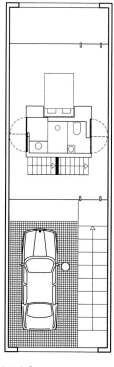

Level 0

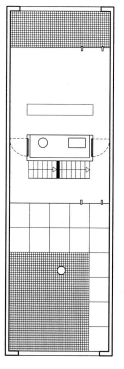

Level 1

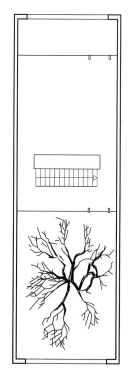

Level 2

The whole interior uses stainless steel. The wall finishings are of white plaster.

The house layout designates each floor for different functions. Thus the rooms share two median walls. Also, they have one glass side on the interior patio, working as a light source and avoiding the feeling of being in a very deep inner space.

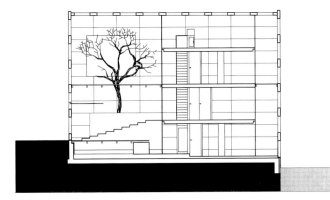

Longitudinal section

Leffe HOUSE

Architect: Studio Archea   **Location:** Leffe, Bergamo. Italy   **Construction Date:** 1998   **Photographs:** Pietro Savorelli, Alessandro Ciampi

The Italian architects at Studio Archea planned each of their activities as occasions to experiment with a diversity of forms and materials.

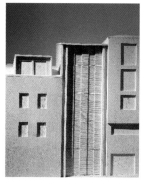

The project, in the historical center of Leffe, near Bergamo, occupies a narrow strip-like site, characteristic of the parceling and urban distribution of this valley.

Architects Laura Andreini, Marco Casamonti, and Giovanni Polazzi founded Studio Archea with the aim of creating "an architecture laboratory for experimental design." They consider each one of their activities an occasion to experiment with a wide range of forms and materials.

The single-family building raised in the Italian town of Leffe replaces a ruined construction in the historical center. It is a way of including in the project the full demolition of the previous structure and making way for a new program drawn up and distributed over different (again new) levels.

Among the particulars that conditioned the site location, the intention of respecting the alignment of the façade is a key factor. It was to adjust to the adjacent fronts, on the street level. Leffe House thus represents itself as a variation of the Gothic style that dominated the place. It is an interplay of planes that fold onto the convex part of the building like the porticos that open and break up the absolute flatness of the façade laid out on the urban elevation.

The dwelling is distributed over the five stories in a repetition of the irregular ground plan. This irregularity just goes right on up the construction, bringing about a succession of surprising interiors, deep perpendicular wells, double-height spaces, and a self-contained elevator shaft. The building's planned volume and the texture of its façades represent the rich design concept and the color scheme not only of the new architecture but of what surrounds it.

In order to create a unique ambience, dissociated from that of the adjacent houses, the façade folds like an accordion. Practically closed and impenetrable, the surface is perforated by a series of long narrow windows that allow the entrance of natural light.

The main street façade, slotted into the space between two buildings of different heights, opens onto the street. A system of shutters of stainless steel and rusted sheet copper close in a single plane that unifies the surface.

The façade –in the same phrasing of long, narrow apertures that look like big venetian blinds– is in Santa Flora stone.

The street façade folds back and forth in a metallic panel system which, at the same time, does not depart from the compositional unity that dominates the building's overall look.

The tower that contains the stair-well fits into the larger space between the complex space created by the periplaral façades of the building.

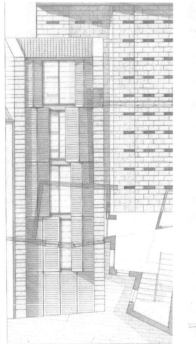

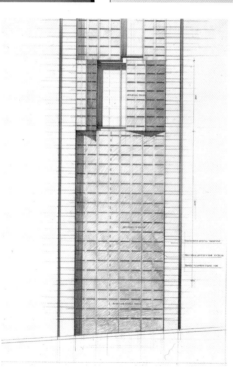

Sketch of elevations

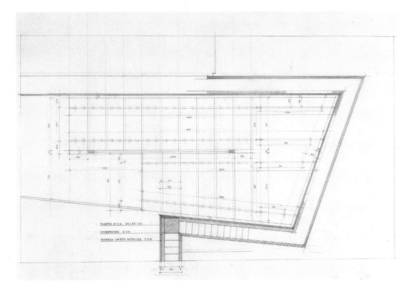

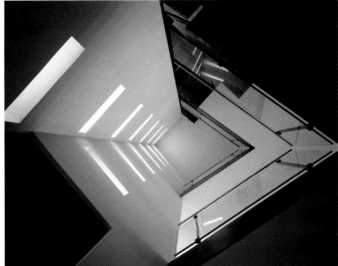

Detail of the stairwell

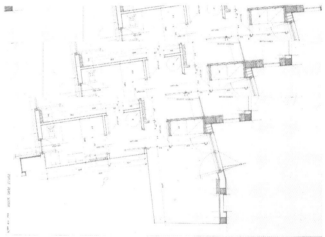

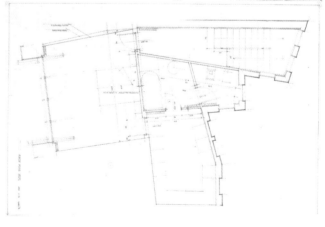

Distribution plans

Allgaier-gaugg HOUSE

Architect: Baumschlager & Eberle   **Location:** Lochau. Austria   **Construction Date:** 1998   **Photographs:** Eduard Hueber

The building style of Allgaier-Gaugg is traditional in Lochau. Stairways go up the mountains, offering a boundless horizon.

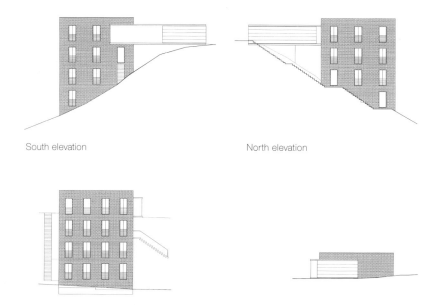

South elevation

North elevation

West elevation

East elevation

The building style of All-gaier-Gaugg is habitual in Lochau. Stairways go up the mountains, offering a boundless horizon. The layout of the sites is narrow, and this, along with the marked incline, makes for buildings that resemble watchtowers along the mountains.

Allgaier-Gaugg's two main structures define it through the plain, contrasting materials used. One of the salient parts unifies all the different functions of the house, from the way it is entered by the upper-level catwalk to the lowest subgrade features. The building's two highest levels are used as living quarters; the lower levels become an individual apartment and a subgrade office.

The priorities defining the different uses of the building are reflected in the differentiating concept in the closure system. While the apartment and the office are accessed from the side, a catwalk on the southern façade beside the garage is used to enter the family unit. The distinctive layout of both areas lies in the different materials used. The building with masonry walls has a cavity wall (ventilated brick); the catwalk is a metal structure below the glassed passageway leading to the main body of the building.

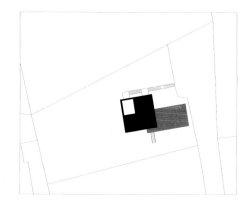

Site plan

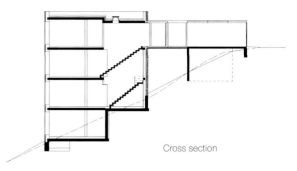

Cross section

The three floors used as living quarters are distinguished by the direct ventilation systems in the kitchens and bathrooms. Both the individual and the family apartments are connected by an interior stairway.

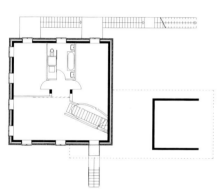

Second floor

Fourth floor

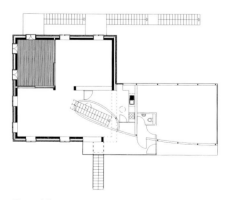

Ground floor

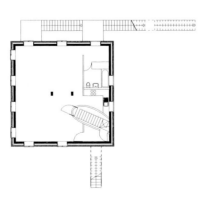

Third floor

440 HOUSE

Architect: Fougeron Architecture   **Location:** Palo Alto, California. U.S.A.   **construction date:** 1999   **photographs:** Richard Barnes

This residence is a clear example of contemporary aesthetics. The house, glassed in and on a free plan, incorporates the latest technologies applicable to building.

This house in Palo Alto, California, is a 4,483-square-foot duplex designed by a couple. It houses two studios, a gym, two bedrooms, and a living room, plus a spare room for family use, the dining room, the kitchen, and a wine cellar.

440 House is a clear example of contemporary aesthetics. The house, glassed in and on a free plan, incorporates the latest technologies applicable to building. These technologies include new glass products from England and cutting-edge framing systems. The exposed steel superstructure (beams, joists, air-conditioning) make it clear that this complex system meets the California seismic codes (it includes seismic damping assemblies). Natural light from different directions (floors, ceilings, walls) is combined with translucent, transparent, and reflecting materials to create visually dynamic spaces.

The house is organized around the central axis, taking in the living room and flanked by the glassed volume and a room used for storage and services. This space was originally conceived as a transparent link between the garden area in back and the front lawn.

The transparency increases through the use of steel framing in conjunction with the glass: it takes its inhabitants right outside. The channel formed by the double-height zone, with glass walls and sand-blasted glass floors, delineates the building. The transparency is again reinforced by the inhabitants' direct contact with the landscape architecture. A bridge crossing the living room connects the rooms on the opposite side.

The whole project was conceived as a conflation of materials, walls, floors, and furniture. The idea was to create a simple stage which, in spite of reductions, would be full of visual surprises and suggestive planes. The result is a way of drawing and building a dwelling type for the coming years.

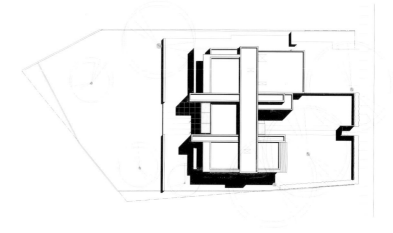

THE NEXT HOUSE

The open plan creates a visual continuity between the living room and the rest of the rooms in the house. The use of translucent materials in the walls contributes to this effect.

Both the longitudinal and the cross sections of the building reflect the spatial continuity that predominates in the design.

Perspective section through the family area

Perspective section through the stairwell

The main staircase, which is made of metal, has its own glassed-in volume. This creates one of the main focuses of the house. The vertical axis here becomes a channel for both natural and artificial light.

THE NEXT HOUSE

1. Entrance
2. Family lounge
3. Living room
4. Dining room
5. Kitchen
6. Garage
7. Studio
8. Guest room
9. Gym
10. Walkway
11. Bedroom
12. Deck

Plan of first floor

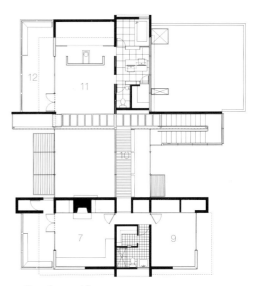

Plan of second floor

in spe HOUSE

architect: Pool Architektur   **location:** Vienna. Austria   **construction date:** March 2000   **photographs:** Hertha Hurnaus

The building achieved the maximum volume possible and, during the design process it was manipulated, reduced and structured in such a way as to create surfaces and spaces adaptable to multiple uses.

The 4,628-square-foot site this single-family house was built on is distinct because of its location on a hill facing north. Other unique features include the fact that the orientation was restricted by being next to another house and not having more than a few yards of separation from the street on the south side. The point of departure for the building's development was to achieve the maximum volume possible. During the design process the building was manipulated, reduced and structured in such a way as to create surfaces and spaces adaptable to multiple uses. The constructed area was finally 1,614 square feet plus the 538-square-foot basement.

The north and south façades connect with the site elevation. The lateral creates a suspended volume that forms the access ramp to the back garage. A set of concrete steps leads down to the entrance area between the basement and zero grade. Following this same line, there is a ramp which, among other things, may be used as a space to park vehicles or to play table tennis.

Entering the house, one is given the impression that one is entering a hill. On one side, the subgrade, there is abundant light from the north; from the opposite side, the house itself may be said to begin at zero grade.

A set of steps above the entranceway enjoys a completely open southern exposure where the hill is. In this ten-foot high space are four steps that lead down to a lower zone that continues into the garden. Through a sliding door, one enters a terrace that opens onto the garden and the pool.

On the opposite side, from the entrance, the work area between the first two levels is accessed. It is a sunny space with views of the rest of the house. Another turn, and a first-floor room opens onto three individual bedrooms, the bathroom, and a small terrace on the south. From there, a steel staircase leads to the roof and marvelous views of Lainzerbach Valley.

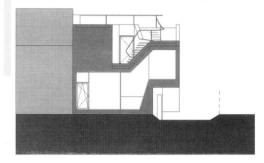

Cross section

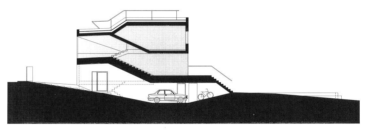

Longitudinal section

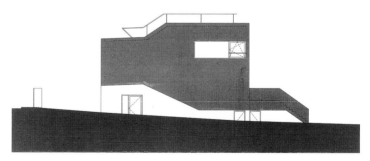

Lateral section

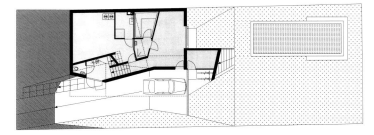

Basement plan

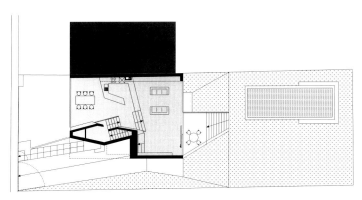

Ground plan

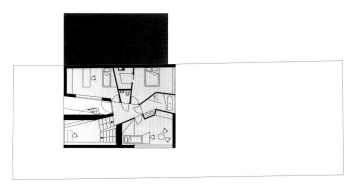

First floor

THE NEXT HOUSE

The house is unique in its zigzag trajectory over the changes in the grade. This peculiarity may also be said to be reflected in the design of the glass apertures in the façades and in the overall conception of the whole space.

The roof becomes an observation point from which to appreciate the magnificent views of the Austrian Lainzerbach Valley.

The perpendicular axis of the house is a visual constant. It is clearly maintained in the stairs and the way the walls and the ceilings capture natural light.

Each section of the staircase is planned independently on each level, establishing a strict relation between the walls and sloping ceilings it connects.

conversion of a STABLE

Architect: Marques & Zurkirchen **Location:** Bergün. Switzerland **Construction Date:** 1994 **Photographs:** Ignacio Martínez

The new form was built with something available in the town itself: wood, with thermal insulation for the needs of this type of low-energy consumption house.

The mural features of his old stable were ratained during the conversion and refitting.

Bergün, a town in Switzerland's Graubünden region, has a pattern of houses laid out side by side toward the center with the stables toward the outskirts.

Conversion of the stables into homes, above all vacation homes, has changed the original character of Bergün, and probably of many other towns as well. All over the world, this type of remodeling work is being observed, with the use of the house varying to include first houses for those who until now have lived in high-density urban areas.

The stable to be refitted was a massive stone-column construction. The mortised larch roof and ceiling architecture included a system of wooden pulley blocks for hauling.

The project retained the original natural stone columns as well as the roof's solid old truss system. The natural protection of the region's traditional architecture would now be used for a new single-family unit. The novelty of the construction lay largely in the new technologies used and the decorative devices,

with the new larch bay fitting precisely into the old stone and protruding toward the town square.

It was built with what was most available in the town itself: wood, with thermal insulation for the needs of this type of low-energy consumption house. The timbering includes an air chamber and galvanized sheet metal elements.

The encounter between the extant frame and the new bay develops on different levels. The use of indigenous materials infuses the project with a traditional spirit, creating a dialogue that includes the renewal of exterior spaces such as balconies and loggias. When all is said and done, great respect has been shown for the original building.

The interface between the different façades brings the massive masonry of the large windowed planes of the old stable together with the echoed motifs in the prefab wood-frame. Thus do tradition and modernity define the next decade's building concepts.

The orientation of the new part of the stable onto the town's original setting contributes to the powerful value of the building in its urban context.

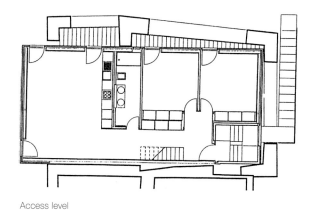

Access level

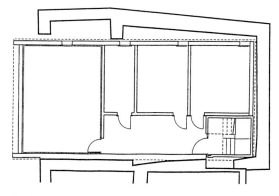

First floor

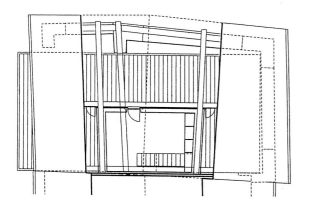

The area beneath the roof

The use of different materials to finish the walls contributes to the modern image of the dwelling. It also distinguishes, without the need of partitions, the different rooms.

The interiors of the new addition were designed according to current needs, without reference to its rural origins.

The new duplex construction, faced in wood, has been set out from the main body, marke by the eave line of the building's hip roof. The convergence of the new part and the older, cleary rural part accentuates the contrast between the two concepts in the traditional town.

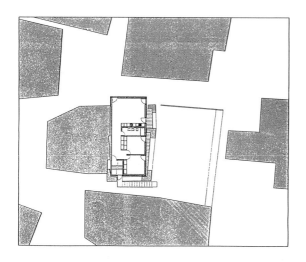

Site plan

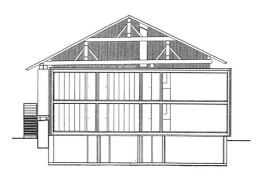

Longitudinal section

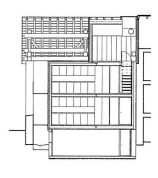

Cross section

One of the façades of the building, perhaps the most urban, is separated from the street grade by scarcely more than three feet and including a light metal stairway. The whole building is intentionally isolated from its settings in this way.

Refurbishing A FARMHOUSE

architect: ARTEC Architekten, Bettina Goetz & Richard Manahl   location: Raasdorf. Austria   construction date: 1998   photographs: Margherita Spiluttini

The renovation and extension of this old farmhouse in Austria serves as a model of how to place elements, shapes, and materials that are typically urban in a rural environment.

The extension project and the shoring-up of the house is a perfect example of the frequent dialogue that takes place between old and new. Traditional architecture may be seen, in this sense, as matching contemporary.

There is also, in this specific case, a confrontation between technology/landscape.

Setting elements, shapes, and building materials typically associated with city living in a rural place is not always easy. This renovation and extension of an old farmhouse in Austria may be seen as a model of how such extrapolation becomes possible if done in a rational way. The only condition imposed by the owner of the house, a farmer and philologist, was that the remodelers should create a space with its own autonomy and that this should be integrated into the environment in such a way as to allow the owner to carry out the two activities comprising his work.

Thus, it was necessary, on the one hand, to design an ambience amenable to working, writing, and reading while, on the other hand, creating a zone separated from this and yet which belonged to the same owner. In this last area, he would carry out the tasks of agriculture originally associated with the place.

There was, then, the question of how to add a vanguardist wing to an older rural construction and fuse the two bodies' diametrically opposed styles harmoniously. It was necessary to avoid an artificial result, one of the main hurdles that the architects carrying out the refurbishing project faced.

The option they chose was that of keeping the existing brick base unit, in the past a stable, and now a living quarters, which was in danger of collapsing. The dilapidated piece was replaced by a shining smooth aluminum facing with veneered wood finishings inside. The element that was to connect the metal bay at the foundation and that unites both constructions is a staircase on one part of the rear façade.

The needs of the occupant also required a renovation that would create spaces for new uses, such as the installation of a heating system, a bathroom, and a reading room.

Some of these new pieces, notably the bath –which is lighted essentially by way of a long narrow skylight and whose shape allows for the conservation of rainwater– were part of the original brick house. Also in the add-on, however, is a reading room that brings a greater sense of privacy. This widens the exterior because it gives immediately onto two terraces, accessed by sliding doors.

The library is the main reason for the extension project. With the surrounding view nearly closed off, apertures in the walls and ceiling channel the light that enters the room.

The staircase connecting two levels is finished in the same sheeting that configures and faces the exterior of the new abstract body.

The bathroom is naturally lit by a long narrow skylight that runs the length of one wall. The skylight section was designed with the secondary function of collecting rainwater.

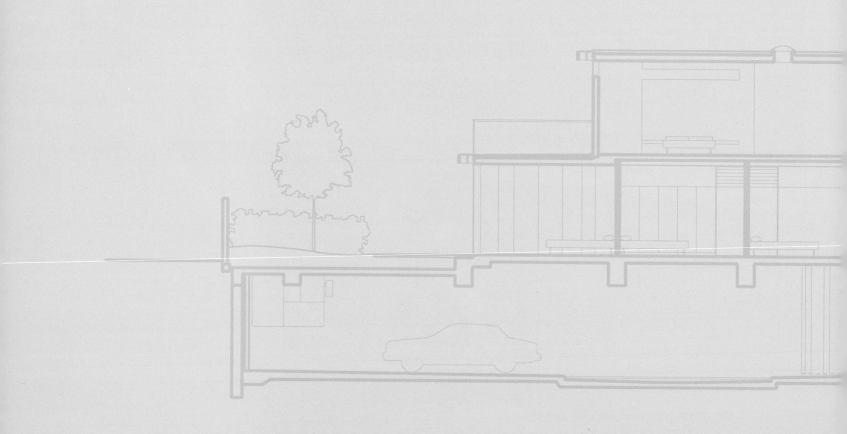

projects

insideouthouse

architect: Sandell Sandberg through Thomas Sandell, Pye Aurell   **initiator**: Wallpaper*   **construction date**: March 2000   **photographs**: Tomasso Sartori

The house is designed to be set into any location and thus adapts equally well to a Swedish woodland or to a place in the Alps or to the English countryside.

The prototype was conceived by Tyler Brûlé, director of the magazine *Wallpaper*, and the architect Thomas Sandell during a barbecue at the journalist's house in Sweden.

Insideouthouse is a living project conceived as a summer residence for a single person or a couple. At the same time, it has enough space to suit a family with children. The concept is, certainly, one of the residential options with the greatest security in regard to the next few years.

From an architectural point of view, the house is on an open plan, with a labyrinthine character. One enters by way of a garden big enough to plant a tree in. The entranceway has a vestibule, and the door gives onto the porch. To the right is the most private part of the house, a large cabin-bedroom and two small ones, each with drawers below the beds, a masonry desk with shelves, a closet with an optional door, and a bathroom with a shower. Another outside bathroom, which is smaller, gives onto the garden.

To the left of the entranceway is the kitchen, with a large window looking onto the porch. Beside the kitchen, the dining area looks onto one of the corners. Farther to the left, the living room opens out into the continually flowing space. At the same time, the exterior walls "continue" inside and the windows "flow on" around the corners. The floor shades into walls, the walls become furniture, which stretches into ceiling.

The idea of the garden is to demarcate an exterior space and turn it into interior. But it keeps on being exterior. The game is one of blurring the inside/outside boundary distinction. The garden creates an intimacy that does not depend on a context because the mobile bungalow is designed to be set into any location and thus adapts equally well to a Swedish woodland or to a place in the Alps or to the English countryside.

A wood-frame structure, it has painted wood façades with plastic elements. The untreated oak walls of the porch and of the outside bathroom continue on into the interior. Inside, the walls, ceiling, and floor are made of pine painted in white. The kitchen and the bath are tiled in white and the bathroom floor is white marble. Both the windows and the ceilings in the bedrooms are painted in yellow, blue, and orange.

WALLPAPER HOUSE

PER INTERNI
1799
Thomas Sandell

Basically designed for a couple, the house can accommodate guests in the small rooms arising out of the outer walls.

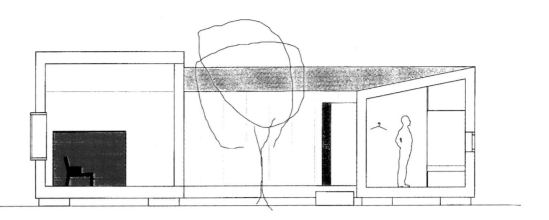

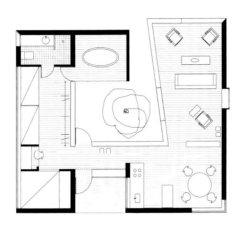

The idea of the patio is to capture the landscape and bring it inside. This is the heart of the project's inside/outside game.

The house folds to create a small patio off which the other rooms open.

Transportable by truck to any point in Europe, this prefab modular home takes four weeks to install and the full cost includes all the materials and labor of the contractors. "For me, it was important to design an all-wood house protected by acrylic panels because it supposes a cultural stigma on traditional material. More important still was my feeling of being in a true refuge into which I could escape."

Thomas Sandell

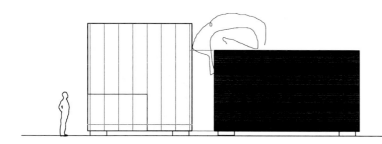

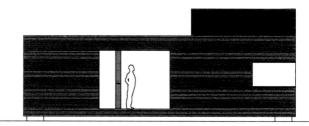

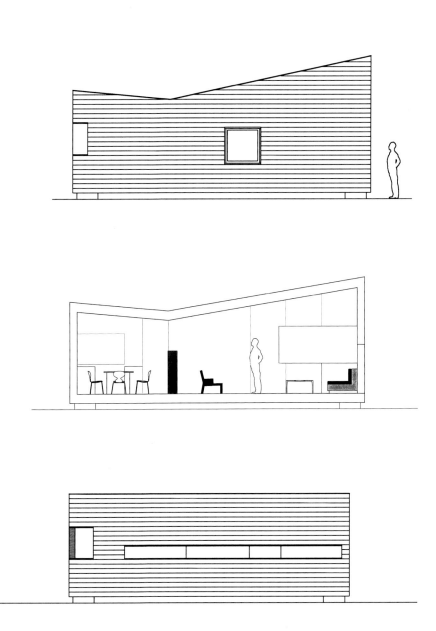

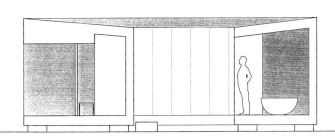

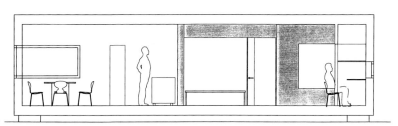

Aronoff HOUSE

Architect: Eric Owen Moss   **Location**: Tarzana, California. U.S.A.   **construction date**: 2004   **photographs**: Paul Groh, Micah Heimlich, Todd Conversano

The house emerges from a conical section at the foot of a hill, and combines spherical and cubical shapes.

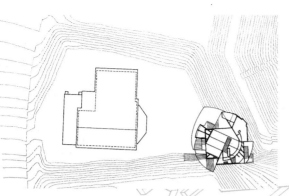

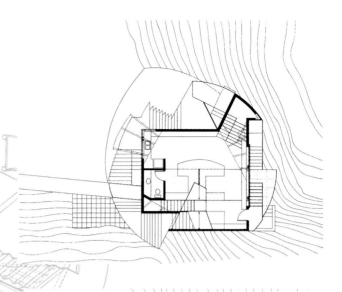

The owners of this house also had a large residence in the northern part of the Santa Monica Mountains, in California. The site of the present house is a narrowing strip northwest of the first one, bounded by a slope in the direction of the Santa Monica Mountains Conservancy, a 4,886-acre nature preserve within a much larger protected district.

This new domestic concept is the apple of the eye of the owners, their employees, guests, and children. The singular structure can be explored, examined, and used as a lookout point because of its location and the configuration of the apartments. The windows maximize the spectacular and varied vistas of the surrounding forest.

The project includes, in addition to the residential areas, a studio, an office, and an apartment. It is situated in a transitional zone on a plane in the upper part of the site, adjacent to the southeastern boundaries of the property. This location makes it easy for those who go to the house exclusively to work to reach it from the road.

The project has three floors. On the highest of these is the studio/office of the owners.

The second floor has an office for three employees; the lowest floor is appointed as a private apartment for the father of one of the owners. The roof, facing the Resource Conservation District of the Santa Monica Mountains and the San Fernando Valley, was built of wood and also has different levels. There are therefore several open-air levels, and they are connected by way of a perimeter stairway as well as an interior stairway to the third floor.

An elevator accesses the apartment on the lowest level. This space has a roof zone on two levels and a patio. It is possible to reach every level from the mezzanine vestibule, or, for that matter, from the exterior.

The house was not conceived as a set of apartments piled up stepwise to adapt to the mountain slope. The idea was to have it emerge from a conical section at the foot of a hill, combining spherical and cubical shapes. These interrelate in a complicated pattern, but they define a very advanced way of building.

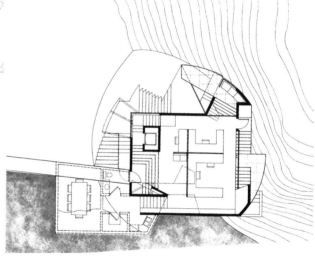

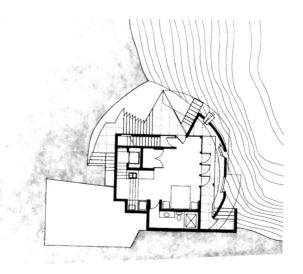

The design system of the roof was conceived as masonry arches that would formalize the roundness of the house.

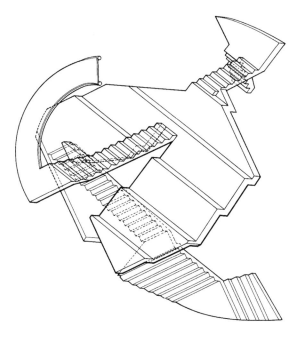

Butterfly HOUSE

Architect: Lippmann Associates   **Location**: Sydney, Australia   **Construction Date**: 1998-2001   **Photographs**: Lippmann Associates

The client insisted that the house should not be subject to a design where straight lines were the norm because this did not correspond to his belief in the principles ruling Feng Shui.

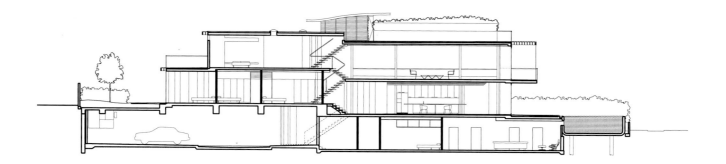

In 1996, Ed Lippmann was invited by a realtor to present the design for his future house on the outskirts of Sydney. Facing north, the place offers some spectacular panoramic views of the city and the harbor to the west.

The client insisted that the house should not be subject to a design where straight lines were the norm because this did not correspond to his belief in the principles ruling Feng Shui, the Chinese discipline that connects the spaces of a building directly with nature.

The project was conceived in a single night and presented the next morning. The client immediately commissioned the work.

The two main curved forms distinguishing the structure pivot around a central body that defines the entranceway and which also contains the stairway that connects the six levels throughout the full trajectory of the house.

The east, or anterior, façade joins the garage to the grade-level story and situates the children's rooms on the upper levels and the master bedroom at the very top of the structure.

The west façade groups in a single unit the kitchen and the dining room on the ground floor along with a mezzanine living room. We might be able to say that this area is the one that enjoys the best views of Sydney Harbor and simultaneously opens onto a patio garden with pool, dominating the west front of the site.

The local authorities rejected the project because it failed to respect the alignment between the neighboring buildings. These latter elements were, inexplicably, planned with their backs to the best views owing to an irrational urban code. Later, the relevant section of the code was modified and the layout of Butterfly House was approved.

The building is a hybrid composition of concrete, steel, and glass. The concrete stiffens the horizontal structure of the steelwork. The metallic elements and an almost imperceptible aluminum section make way for the interface between each of the levels. They also open up the space to the large glass panels sheathing the piece. Steel-to-steel joints supporting the glass panels are sealed with silicon.

Some of the most advanced technical systems have been used here to achieve the curved, sliding glass skin as well as the projecting cornices to protect from direct solar radiation while allowing heat accumulation and maximum natural lighting in all the spaces.

The rationale behind the intermediate form of the floor-to-floor layout is related to a smooth form of going up and down to harness the different views and energies in the immediate environment, including the best orientations toward the sun.

Access level

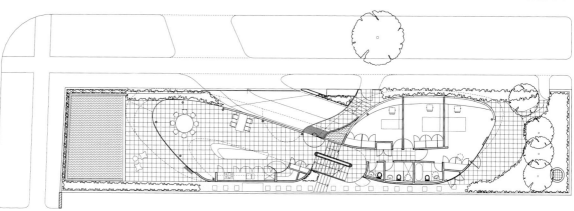

The building is made of a concrete structure that uses large projecting cornices as terraces. The metallic parts of the sheathing interface with the concrete parts and support the large glass panels in the façades.

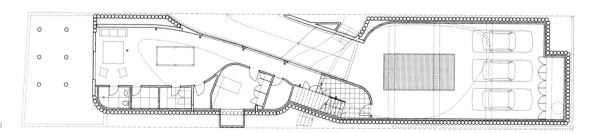

Plans of the study and the garage

Belvedere Residence

Architect: Fougeron Architecture **Location:** Belvedere, California. U.S.A. **Construction Date:** In design phase, projected for 2002 **Photographs:** Fougeron Architecture (maquette and renderings)

This Belvedere, California residence, a 6,458-square-foot design, is still in the design phase.

The building breaks up the natural topography as it fits into the landscape: terraces are created and a wide-windowed façade.

In order to take advantage of the magificent views and integrate the house into the landscape, the siting is on a slightly inclined terrain. Two containing walls create a rise on which the living space is set, light and transparent.

The walls narrow the site and continue from the outside of the house to the inside. Wherever they are, they reinforce the relationship: the different levels are linked solidly both visually and physically.

On the back of the site, an excavation next to the first wall gives rise to a striking entranceway sequence backed up by the magnificent landscape gardening. Crossing the walkway over the garden in the direction of the main door, the proprietors will see themselves surrounded by trees, the sound of water along the garden wall, and views of the Golden Gate Bridge (through the translucent marble staircase).

The large volumes containing the dining room and the living room are located above the back wall. The floor-to-ceiling glass façade creates beautiful views. The glassed-in area containing the office is also slotted into this space, accessible from the interior staircase as well as the exterior walkway.

The office is on the third floor, which is also on grade level. The main living spaces are on the second floor, and the bedrooms are on the lowest level. All of these spaces are directly accessed from outside.

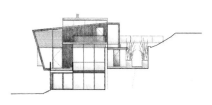

East façade

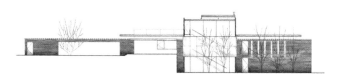

North façade

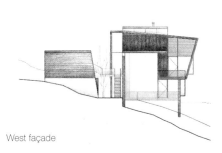

West façade

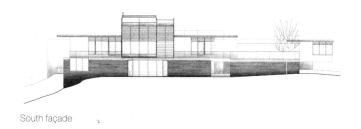

South façade

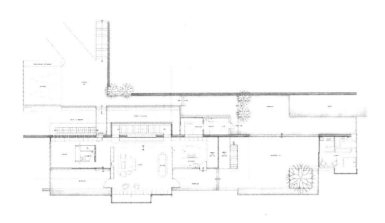

Grade level

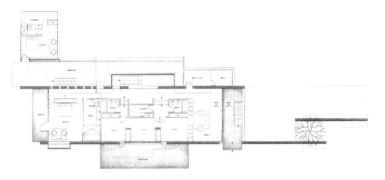

Level 1

The whole house projects the rooms in an exterior orientation, enriching the different views.

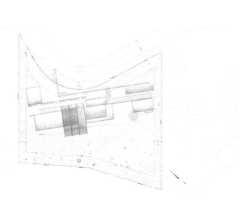

Site plan

Beacon Street HOUSE

architect: Fougeron Architecture   **Location:** Beacon Street, San Francisco. U.S.A.   **construction date:** 2004   **photographs:** Fougeron Architecture

Temporal is the perception of the passage
of time one has from the house through the
contrasts each season produces in the urban landscape.

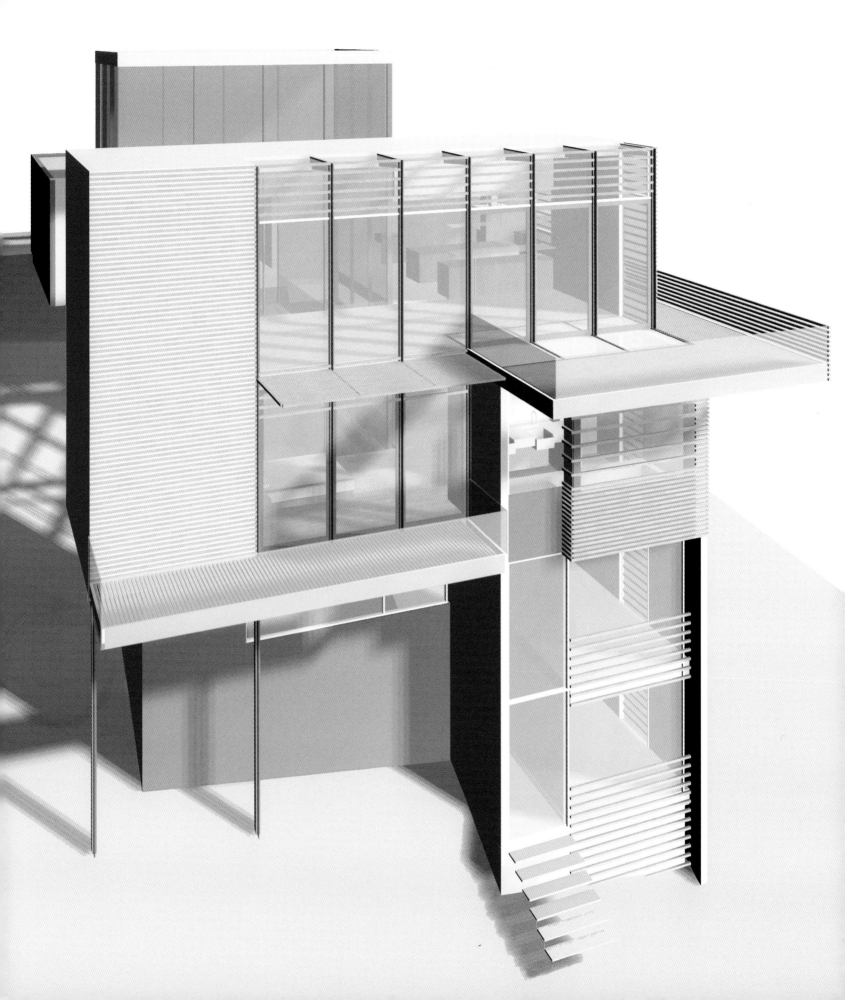

Fougeron Architecture is a renowned North American firm whose work reveals a strong compromise by the clarity of its proposals, the integrity of its designs, and the quality of architectural details. The founder of the firm, the architect Anne Fougeron, directs the professional practice of her studio in search of the perfect balance between the idea of architecture and the final form taken on by the constructed building. Her work, as may be seen in the Beacon Street House, can be defined by three basic premises: that the architectural space should be modulated by the quality and the characteristics brought about by natural light; that any innovation applied to the structure should become architectural ornamentation; and, finally, that the exploration of the visual and tactical character of the materials should make its inhabitants able to enjoy the building.

The program in the Beacon Street edifice consists in remodeling and extending a residence on a San Francisco hill with spectacular panoramic views of the bay and downtown of San Francisco.

The building's conception is founded on three concepts, namely, perpendicularity, transparency, and temporality.

The last-named concept is applied to the project by fitting the steep incline of the site on which the building is set by means of different mechanisms such as glass flooring, or a light stairway, tucked like an elevator into a glass shaft.

The transparency comes about when, in each, an invisible transition is produced between the interior space and the exterior of the dwelling.

Temporal is the perception of the passage of time one has from the house through the contrasts each season produces in the urban landscape.

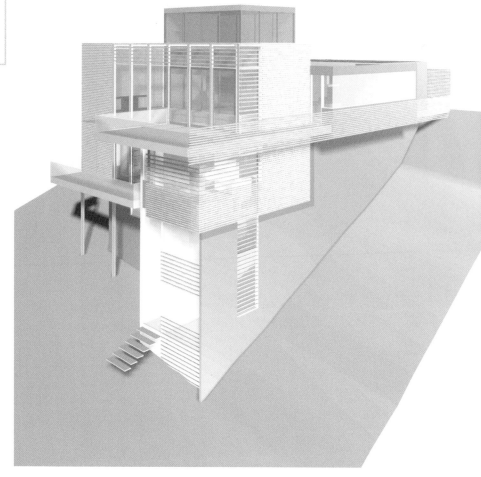

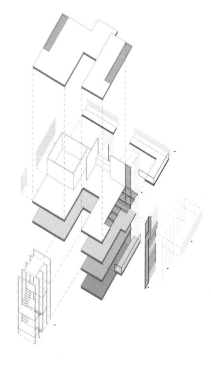

transparency

verticality

temporality

The access level of the house is on grade level, where the day-use rooms are located (kitchen, dining room, living room). The lower floor contains the bedrooms.

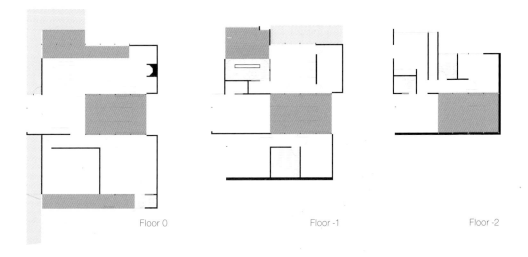

Floor 0   Floor -1   Floor -2

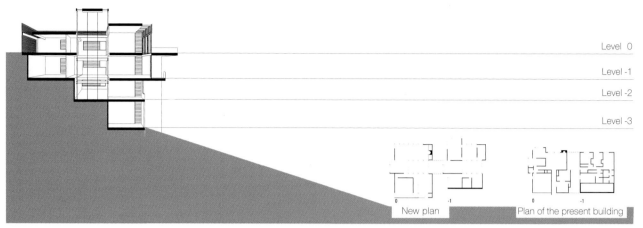

Level 0

Level -1

Level -2

Level -3

Level 0: Entranceway, study, kitchen, dining room, living room

Level -1: General rooms and bathrooms

Level -2: Guest rooms and bathroom

Level -3: Gym and storeroom

New plan

Plan of the present building

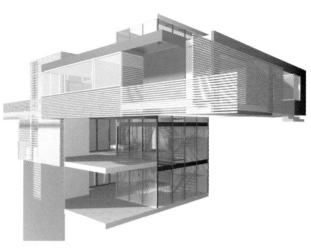

From any room it is possible to enjoy the panoramic view the privileged site provides.

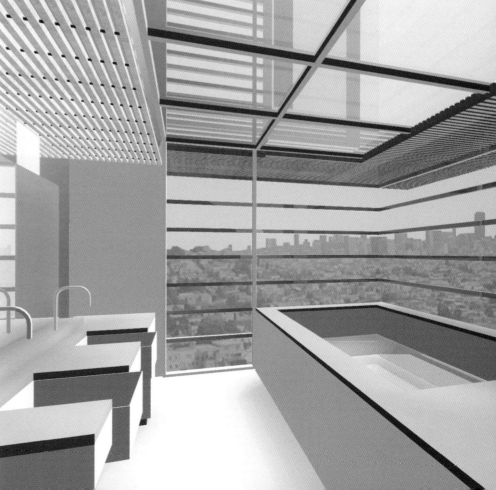

wooster street LOFT

architect: Archi-tectonics   **location**: Wooster Street, SoHo, New York. U.S.A.   **construction date**: 1998   **photographs**: Paul Warchol

The Wooster Street project consisted of turning a fifth-floor apartment in a remodeled SoHo building into a living space for an art collector.

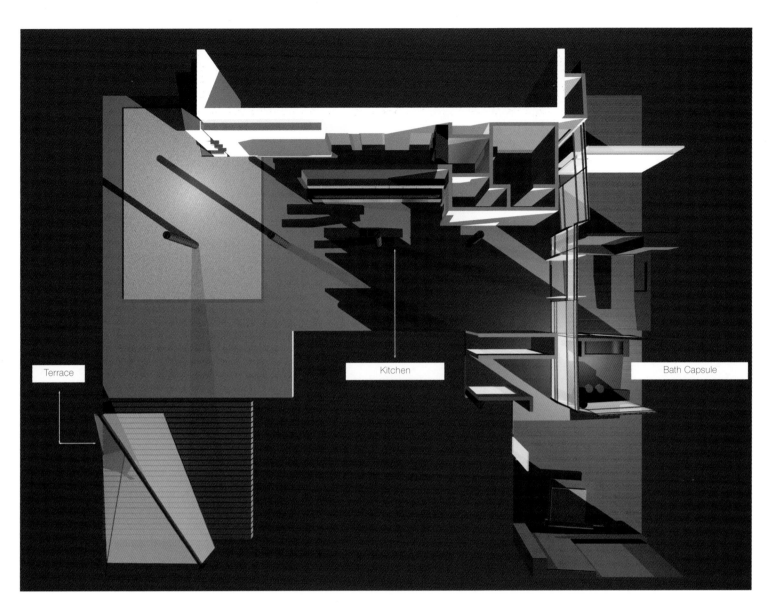

Terrace

Kitchen

Bath Capsule

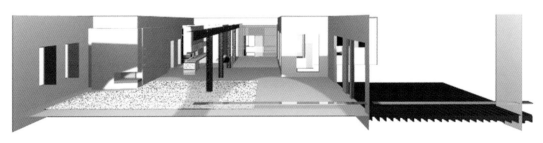

The Wooster Street project consisted of turning a fifth-floor apartment in a remodeled SoHo building into a living space for an art collector. Given the fact that the proprietor was constantly traveling between London and New York, the Internet became the main line of communication.

The apartment that defines this project appears to be a loft, an existing and manipulable space. Doing it over again with additions and divisions meant reformulating the domestic elements for the creation of space flow and continuity. The loft's design generated different zones with three uses stipulated: public, private, guest. And the general concept relates these concepts and links them. The division plans of the rooms become transparent, slippery, pivotal membranes.

The kitchen is defined by a dividing wall that folds back and suspends the work surfaces. The molded aluminum of the walls turns into a kind of cabin modulation. Inside, we find two suspended, cornice-like work islands and a third fixed one of cement and polyurethane that turns on the breakfast pivot. The presence of a hearth as something with its own identity is separated from the wall and made the central visual focus.

The bathroom is a floating capsule whose functions are integrated to form a single sweeping element surrounded by glass panels. This supposes physical separations and no visual separations in the space, with showers that are seen and heard as such.

Finally, the house contains fields with different functions, always retaining that continual flowing sweep of space, with the salient textures in what are screens more than walls.

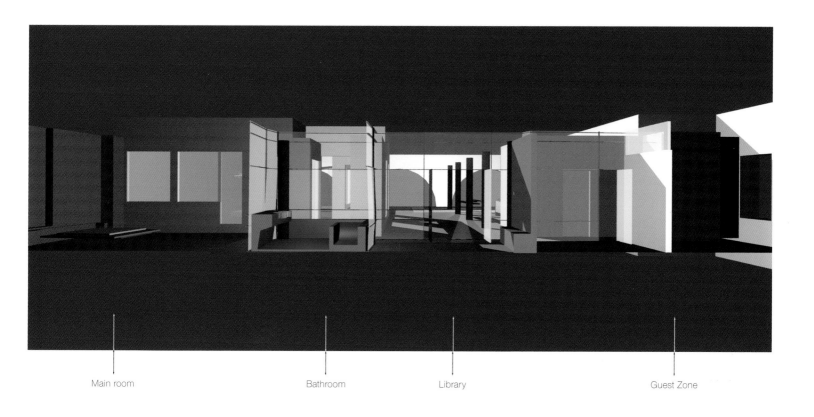

Main room   Bathroom   Library   Guest Zone

The domestic program is organized in "occupation fields" or places where determined activities are generated. These fields may be private, public, or for guest use. Such is the way of classifying the use of space as conceived by the architect.

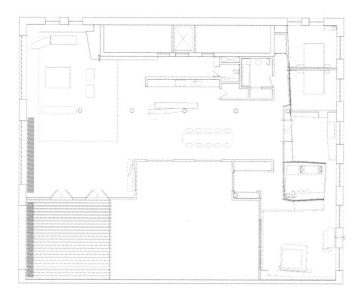

In the floor plan, the capsules may be appreciated in their function of making the bathrooms separate from the perimeter walls.

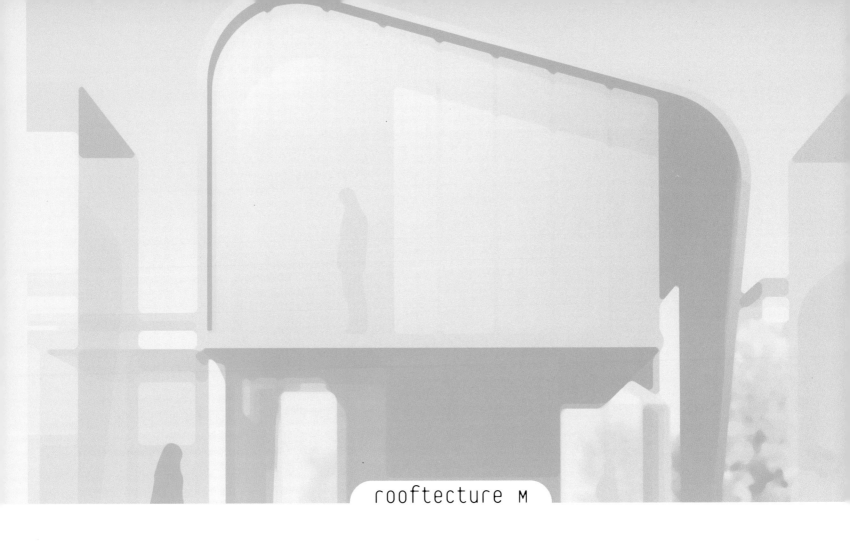

rooftecture M

Architect: Shuhei Endo Architect Institute   **Location**: Osaka. Japan   **Construction Date**: 1999

Rooftecture M is a project that suggests a chair shape for a house and workshop under construction in a small city three hours by train from Osaka.

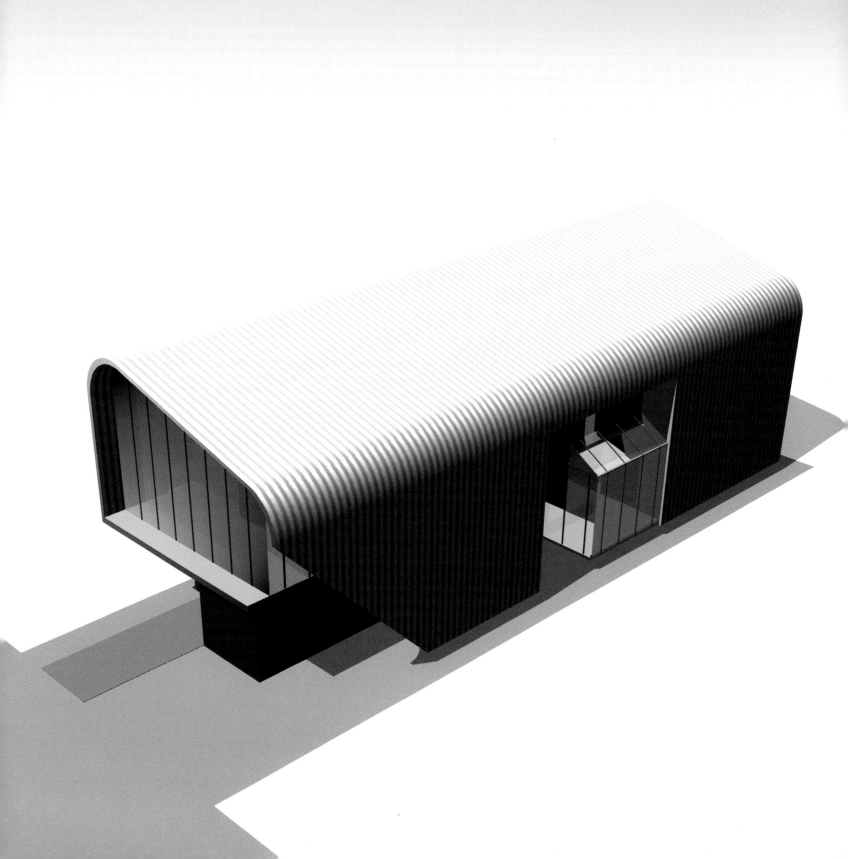

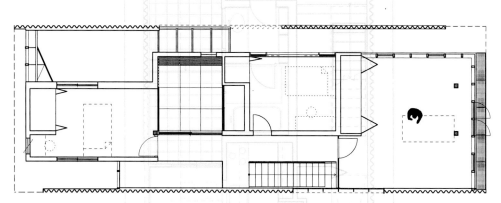

First floor plan

On the first floor, the rooms, including the studio, or workshop, are organized on the north front of the building, where a homogeneous illumination is ideal for working.

Rooftecture M is a project that suggests a chair shape for a house and workshop under construction in a small city three hours by train from Osaka, Japan, on a site that is not very large, but flat and in an attractive residential zone.

The ground plan of the house-workshop is rectangular, with rounded lines on the north and the south sides.

Including a workshop capable of handling a great influx of visitors was one of the initial requirements of the owner. This was the way in which the architects were requested to construct a series of spaces that would respect the quietness of the place and not attract attention from the street, in spite of the visits.

The workshop is in the northern section of the second floor, looking onto the street and located above the bathroom, the laundry room, and a second bathroom on the ground floor.

The dining room-living room is also on the ground floor, and has enough space to allow for comfortable family gatherings. This bay also admits abundant light and enjoys good ventilation.

The configuration of the house is due to the continuation, free of angles, of the lateral wall and the roof. This idea of continuity in space is the architect's response to keeping it inside as a place for family meetings.

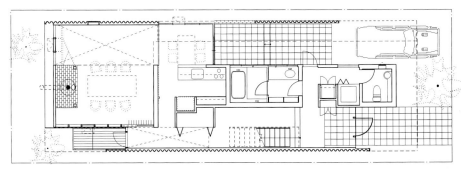

Ground floor plan

The roof becomes the main motif of the architecture. The building's entire cladding creates economical features that aim to save space for the carefully organized bays inside.

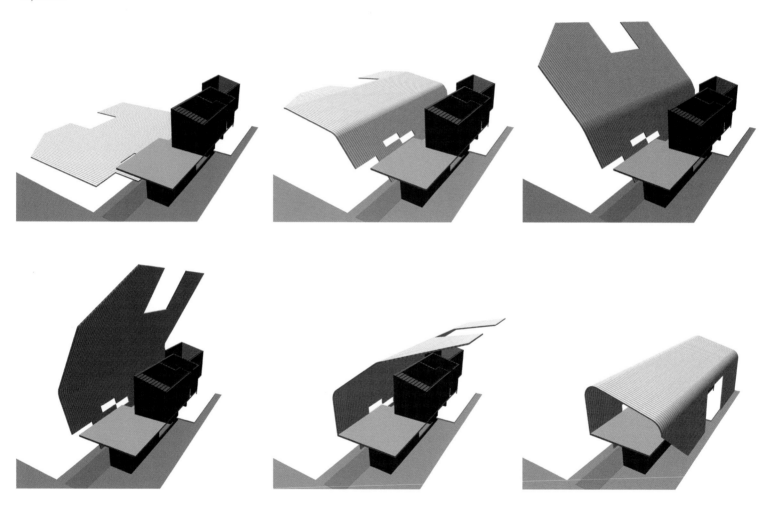

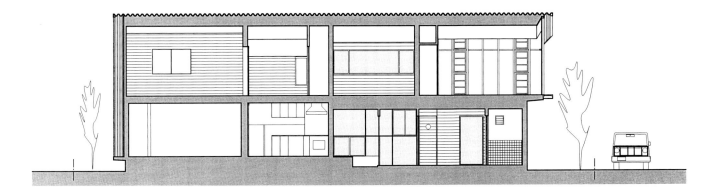

Longitudinal section

Inside, the rooms succeed each other independently. The interfaces between them takes up minimal space, aided by the singularity of the roof-façade skin.

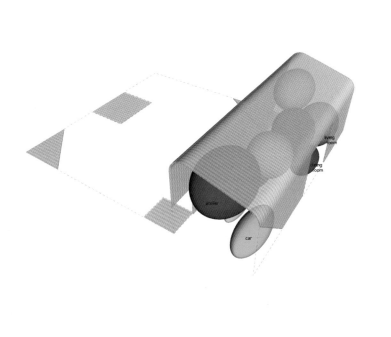

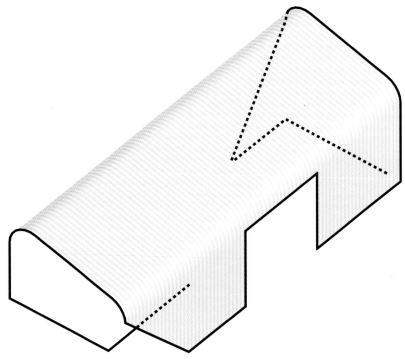

the Digital HOUSE

architect: Hariri & Hariri, Gisue Hariri & Mojgan Hariri. Project sponsored by "House Beautiful"   **Location:** A piece of land of 2,5 acre   **construction Date:** 1997-1999

This project for a studio explores the nature of
domestic space in the new millennium by examining
the structure of the family.

Due to the global revolution, architecture of the new millennium will have to bring into the home the activities that are going on outside of it: work, shopping, education, entertainment, and physical exercise. Within this concept, the Digital House was conceived as a prototype to examine the architecture of the new millennium.

This project for a studio explores the nature of domestic space in the new millennium by examining the structure of the family, our changing habits, the institution of marriage, children, and the new technologies of communication and information.

The house is organized around a steel frame roofed in glass that incorporates the use of a microelectronic technology of amorphous materials building up fine transparent plates into an active panel. These high-definition panels are in use by the NASA and in military aviation.

In the Digital House, the architecture involving the main bays has been cut down to simple and efficient, partially prefabricated spaces. These units come off the main structure like the spaces of an industrial building. In contrast with the three prefab bedrooms, office and school, and living room-dining room and kitchen, digitally connected to the piece, there are also transitional (circular) interspaces for people to momentarily disconnect. They thus move from virtual- to real-world tasks, contemplating their physical skills and their spiritual well-being.

This is on a nearly 2.5-acre suburban site on a slight rise and near an artificial lake. The real landscape is the low-maintenance lawn with lines of trees bordering the parterres. The virtual landscape, on the other hand, offers many possible views from the house.

The work spaces are walled in liquid crystal, replacing the individual monitors. Hence, the children's work rooms or classrooms are connected to schools all over the world, which can be followed continually.

The living room, located upstairs, is the place of entertainment and leisure. Any film or TV program is globally accessible and can be seen from a downy, organic, comfortable sofa.

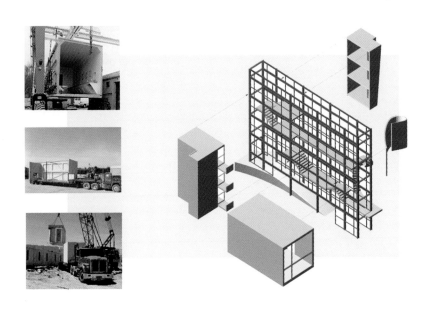

SITE PLAN

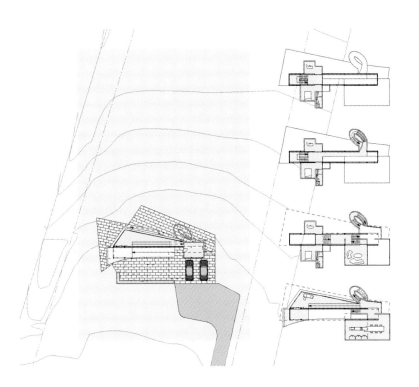

The kitchen-dining room operates like a laboratory. It also connects to the main structure of the house. Meals can be prepared as in our favorite restaurant with the help of a virtual chef, we can dine with a guest or friend (also virtual) through a liquid crystal wall.

All the bedrooms are equipped with a machine to record dreams, so you can see them again on the liquid crystal wall of the room any time you wish.

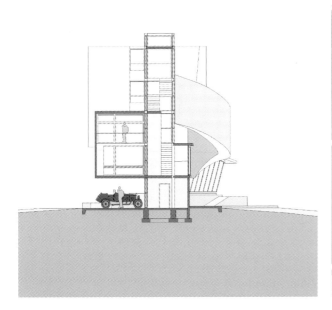

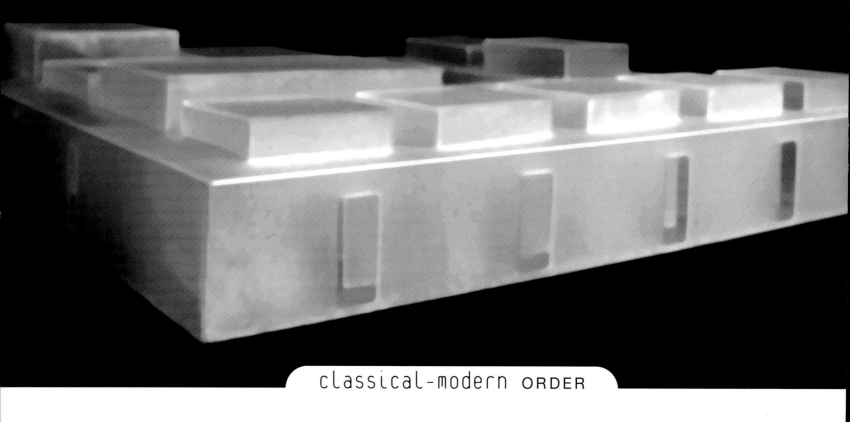

classical-modern ORDER

architect: Aires Mateus & Associates   Location: Portugal   construction Date: 2000   photographs: Aires Mateus & Associates

The generation of architects born in the '60s have had the chance to work and build their own projects and also to complete their training by collaborating in the studios of their teachers.

Architects' work reflected in
wood and fiber maquettes.

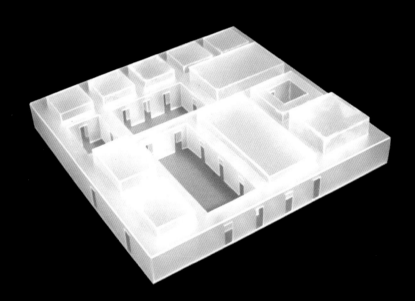

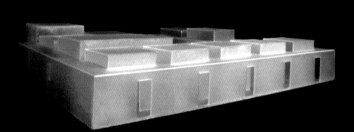

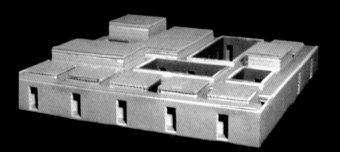

The brothers Francisco and Manuel Aires Mateus (born in 1963 and 1964 respectively) make up this architecture studio whose activity has developed out of an acquired experience inherited from the masters of Portuguese architecture. Regular collaborators in the recent work of architect Gonçalo Byrne, the two brothers' academic experience, acquired in the innovative Portuguese schools of architecture, helps to put them up among the most promising of the new generation of professional architects "constructing" the landscape in Portugal.

In the words of architect Nuno Portas, "There was a time when it was easy to create a critical and coherent story about the architecture done in Portugal. Maybe because architect-authors were few in number and (well) renowned... But the urban crisis of the developmentalist models of the '60s and '70s came about when they grew more and more critical of the proliferation of the post-Venturi and Rossi trends. The coincidence of

that critical moment with the democratic changes in the Iberian countries explains that dominance of the discourse on the urban expression of the new local policies. It is contradictory that that same context would see the rise of very disparate architectural trends and that the recovering city would become the scene of a new eclecticism...

It is a contradiction that the State has recently offered unsuspected opportunities through restricted compe-titions or consultations, whether to mature architects who had gone years without commissions (Tainha, Távora, Siza, Vasconcelos and Cabral, Soutinho, Figuereido, etc.) or to other people of the subsequent generations (de Burne and Ramalho, Carrillo de Graça, Souto de Moura, Cortesao, or Graça Dias)."

On the other hand, the Lisbon and Oporto schools have also come into a golden age while letting the best professionals in the country work in an academic environment. Also contributing

to this is the rise of the balancing effect supposed by the funds for infrastructure coming from the European Union.

All of this has provided the generations of architects born in the '60s with the opportunity to work and build their own projects as well as completing their training collaborating in the

studios of their teachers, as is the case with the Aires Mateus brothers.

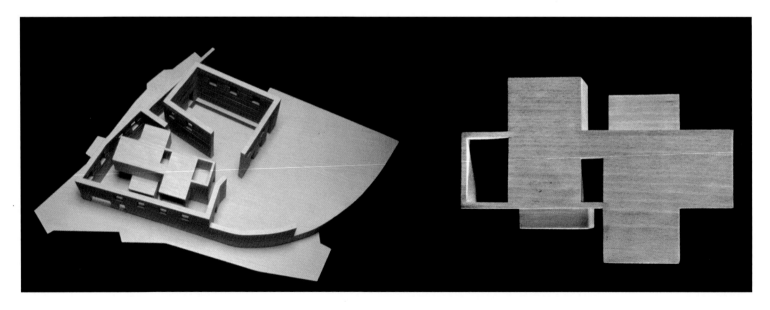

It is interesting to read this architecture, committed and affirmative,
in the same way we read that of
architect Gonçalo Byrne, although
the latter with a more acute sense
of the classical-modern.

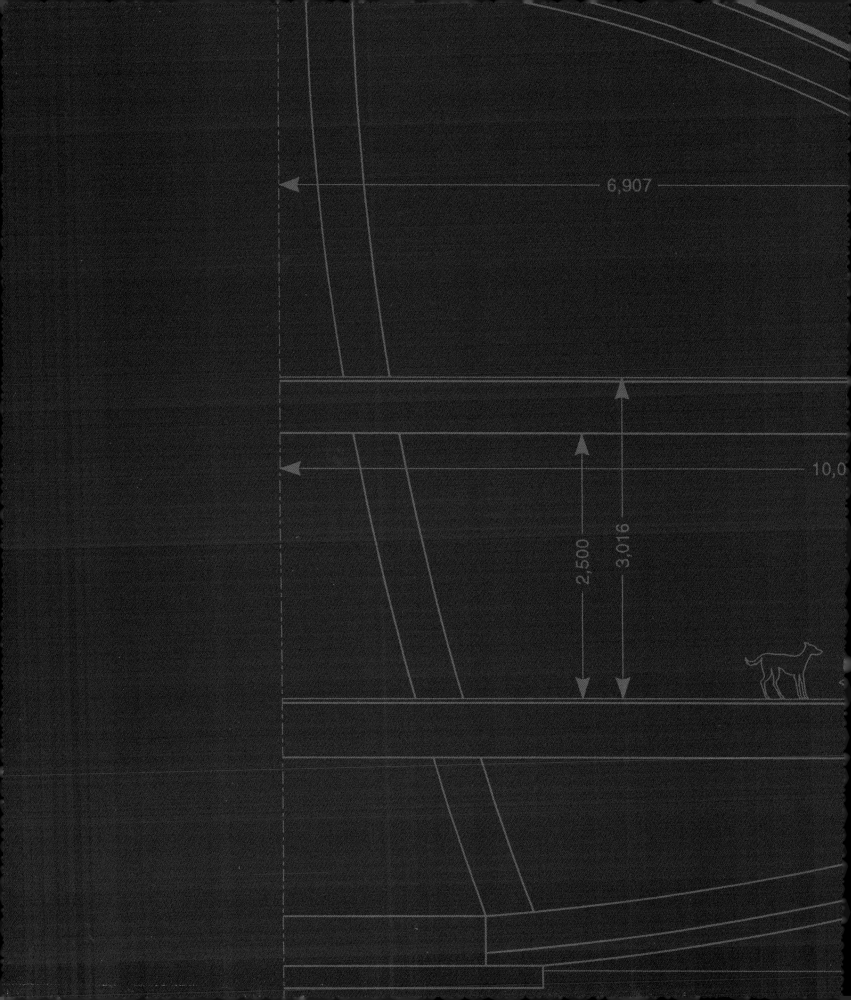

epilogue

DOMES: an alternative for the future

Architect: Patrick Marcilli   **photographs:** Miquel Tres

For centuries human beings have sought a personal private space in which to conduct their daily life. This desire to have a house, one's own house, has always remained with us. This is the materialization of an intimate place where we may give free rein to our emotions, dreams, and feelings and where our lives can be lived in a pleasant and comfortable way. We want to do this while applying to this space creative concepts that make our lives easier.

The perspective of this space goes further, then, than the simple idea of refuge. The house, the home, is also a place of shelter, a construction conceived with the aim of realizing and showing the social aspirations of its inhabitants. It is the carrier of traditions, and its design is markedly defined by the aesthetic, cultural, and economic needs of a specific time and place.

Without a doubt, the twentieth century was the century of the house, one which distanced itself from the large-scale and approached human concerns to direct its aspirations to creating solutions. The typical problems of shape, function, materials, and space must be solved to bring a domestic logic and a comfort into our homes.

A look at the domestic architecture of the twentieth century points to a diversity that makes it difficult to speak of a concrete style, a single trend. This richness of differences, this plurality, is what makes it possible for the most traditional structures to share space with other domestic buildings that are more attractive because of the singularity of their features, yet equally

effective. In fact, the influence of those older models is often apparent in the design of more contemporary dwellings.

The technological advances and the application of new materials and resources, true motivating energies in the construction solutions of the twentieth century, have brought these changes to a greater number of people. Aware of this revolution, silent and slow, but profound, Domespace (domespace.com) offers a new concept in housing.

This new way of understanding the house takes ideas from the past and explores and redefines them with new variations adapted to current needs. Traditional elements are recovered and established in a new context, reinterpreted in a variety of shapes and materials.

Paradoxically, this new millennium, swallowed up by technologies and industries that advance at ever more dizzying paces, is crying out for a return of our dwellings to nature and traditional materials like wood, brick, or stone. It is a cry that has gained support; materials that are today considered to be the most ecological, warm, and natural.

Domespace is a good example of making it possible to conceive new shapes from old through industry's technical advances. The lens-shaped form is hardly new: in all times and places we have used the circular shape in our buildings. From the igloo to the wickiup, passing through different kinds of religious buildings, the circle has always been present in human life, a constantly repeated geometrical figure.

Domespace is a construction that is usually of wood. Both inside and outside, cedar, beech, or pine have been used for their warmth and durability. The ecological, natural, recyclable, resistant nature of wood combined with the new treatments currently marketed and contemporary building technologies make it even more efficient.

The concept of protection and greater comfort that Domespace offers is carefully studied. The designs guarantee great security and unique insulation. The dome withstands earthquake tremors, strong winds, storms, cold, heat. It is the ideal refuge from the outside world, yet it maintains contact with the environment into which we set it in a kind of adaptation.

This way of understanding the home represents an attempt to harmonize the pure line and the simple (but not easy) shape. The reductionist view, cleanly ornamented, and the new industrial resources available adapt this timeless style to nature and landscape. It is a relaxed and fruitful dialogue with the environment, respect for the ecosystem. Domespace is the story of the wood house returning to the future.

Thus, with Domespace comes a new generation of smart houses that avoid the rigidity of the straight line. Domes shun the traditional design body, which can be visually aggressive, they oust this from modern architecture and promote gentle, relaxing lines. Domespace returns, as it were, to the architectural features natural to other regions and countries and, from the most modern interpretation of concepts that have more than proved their value in solving building problems, adapts them to any modern topology and need.

Domespace

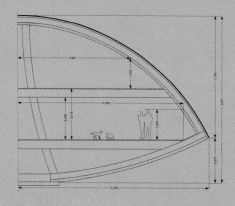

Built entirely of wood, the Domespace design fits naturally into the landscape in a kind of mimicry. The house joins the terrain –it is projected in such a way as to guarantee the absolute security of its inhabitants. The curved shapes offer an effective protection against all kinds of weather conditions. The structure is cyclone resistant because the curve offers practically no wind resistance. It is earthquake resistant because it resists movements of up to magnitude 8 on the Richter scale.

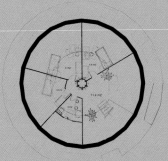

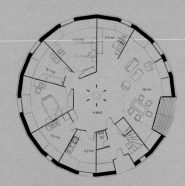

The lenticular structure Dome-space uses makes it possible–thanks to a rotatory crown incorporated in some models of this building–for the building to turn on its own central axis. This guarantees optimal natural illumination and makes it possible to constantly change the view of the landscape from inside the house.

Like the exterior, the interior of the dwelling is wood. In this case the materials chosen are beech, oak, and pine. It is a recyclable material, refinishable and ecological, and it is tremendously resistant, insulating, warm and natural.

No two Domespace interiors are the same. This is true simply because needs, preferences, and resources differ among the company's clientele. The organization of the living spaces is designed according to the desires of each owner.

La Martire

The singular curving shapes, halfway between the igloo and the hut, bring the building into minimal contact with the terrain on which it is set. Thus, the house is insulated from humidity and becomes a healthy and comfortable space.

virgine peron

DOME FERCOT

Unlike traditional cubical designs, Domespace maximizes the space devoted to living. The circular form allows optimal interior organization to free what would otherwise be dead space for use in installing storage elements and tailor-made furniture.

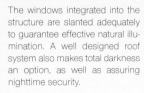

The windows integrated into the structure are slanted adequately to guarantee effective natural illumination. A well designed roof system also makes total darkness an option, as well as assuring nighttime security.